AF816531

THE 2022 ANNUAL

Hepburn

The Best of 2022

Articles and Interviews from 20 Amazing Business Women

10 Ellen Media

Copyright © 2022 Jacqueline Hodges & 10 Ellen Media

All rights reserved.

No portion of this book may be reproduced in any form without written permission from the publisher or author, except as permitted by Australian copyright law.

This publication is designed to provide accurate and authoritative information in regard to the subject matter covered. It is sold with the understanding that neither the author nor the publisher is engaged in rendering legal, investment, accounting or other professional services. While the publisher and author have used their best efforts in preparing this book, they make no representations or warranties with respect to the accuracy or completeness of the contents of this book and specifically disclaim any implied warranties of merchantability or fitness for a particular purpose. No warranty may be created or extended by sales representatives or written sales materials. The advice and strategies contained herein may not be suitable for your situation. You should consult with a professional when appropriate. Neither the publisher nor the author shall be liable for any loss of profit or any other commercial damages, including but not limited to special, incidental, consequential, personal, or other damages.

ISBN: 978-0-6457075-0-2

9 8 7 6 5 4 3 2 1 edition 2022

For the women
who seek a successful path in life, and in business

AND

For Alexander,
who encourages me every step of the way and endures my immersion into Hepburn ever so patiently.

Hepburn

THE 2022 ANNUAL

ACKNOWLEDGEMENT

To all the wonderful women who have contributed to this creation of the annual edition of Hepburn.

Thank You.

10 ELLEN MEDIA
proudly brings you

Hepburn

Magazine

Editor-in-Chief
Jacqueline Hodges

Editorial Enquiries

07 2139 8128

10 Ellenborough House,
126 Brisbane Street, Top of the Town, Ipswich, QLD 4305

hm@10ellenmedia.com

Advertising

sam@10ellenmedia.com

10 ELLEN MEDIA

Hepburn Magazine is published by 10 Ellen Media
ABN: 22 110 673 604}

Articles express the opinions of the authors and not necessarily those of Hepburn or 10Ellen Media. The Hepburn privacy policy is located at https://hepburnmag.co/privacy-policy/

10 Ellen Media's privacy notice can be read at:

https://10ellenmedia.com/privacy-policy/

Annual Issue

Photography & illustrations:

Unsplash, Pexels, Phil Whitehouse, Vishnubonam, Drmobs

Cover Image: Jacqueline Hodges

Contributors

Jacqueline Hodges, Julia Jerg, Rebecca Mdgregor, Isabella Stephan, Georgie Arnaud

About Hepburn

When life gives us lemons, Hepburn is the cocktail. It is a Swiss chocolate in times of stress, a glass of wine after a long day, and a pedicure date with a best friend.

Hepburn is a fresh approach to a women's magazine. We celebrate strong, fearless, and ambitious women who are born to lead with power and dignity.

Our content is crafted for sophisticated Hepburn women for whom the sky is not the limit, it is just the beginning.

Hepburn inspires women to cherish their 'me' time in luxury.

Connect with us

Join in the conversations about the latest issues that affect your life on the Hepburn Magazine Instagram and Facebook page.

Video Interviews

Subscribe to our Hepburn YouTube channel to watch the latest In Conversation series with Amazing Australian and Aspiring Australian Women.

Podcast

Subscribe to our Hepburn podcast on Spotify to hear the selected articles and the latest In Conversation series with Amazing and Aspiring Australian Women.

Website

Visit hepburnmag.co to find out more

Phone

Call us on 0481 999 673 Monday to Friday between 9:00am and 8:00pm AEST.

STAY TUNED
Subscribe

Forward

Hello and welcome to the first of our annual editions, The 2022 Annual Edition of Hepburn.

Hepburn magazine is a monthly business and lifestyle magazine written with women in mind. We bring articles, interviews and stories across our seven sections: Flourish, Appetence, Abundance, Ambition, Amore Propre, Passion, and Leisure.

When I first started Hepburn in 2020, I wanted to create a magazine to inspire and empower women. Since then we have grown from a bi-monthly into a monthly magazine. We have featured amazing women from Australia and Abroad, and Remembered those women who have stood tall and steadfast in their own time.

During 2022, we have had the great pleasure of bringing our readers stories, articles, and interviews from many amazing women throughout the year. With this edition, we now bring you a collection of our interviews and guest articles and shine the light on 20 amazing women whom we featured during 2022.

Each of these women are amazing in their own right and our stories provide a small glimpse into their triumphs, their courage, how their actions forged a pathway for others to follow, and how they share their knowledge to inspire others to be the best. We wish you great enjoyment and inspiration as you flip through the pages and read each article.

So, as the year closes, I welcome you and invite you to read the inaugural Annual Edition of Hepburn.

Wishing you a very happy, healthy and successful year in 2023.

Relax. Enjoy. Be Inspired.

Jacqueline Hodges

Contents

Ambition

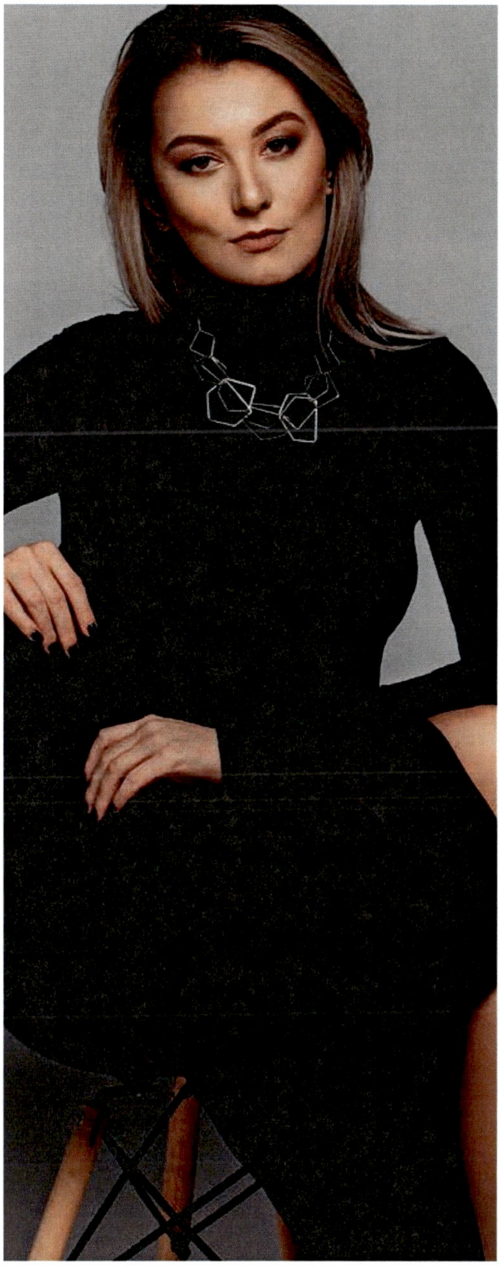

Pg 59

Flourish

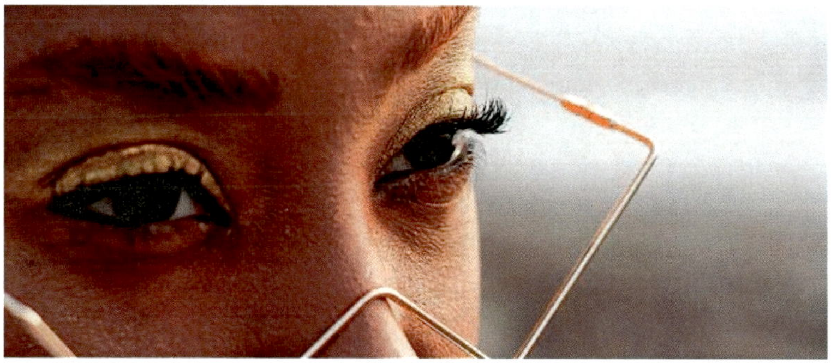

Pg 10

Appetence

Pg 27

Abundance

Pg 44

Amour Propre

Pg 74

Passion

Pg 101

Leisure

Pg 114

Hepburn

Buy your digital issues at www.hepburnmag.co

Hepburn

Buy your digital issues at www.hepburnmag.co

Flourish

1. Grow or develop in a healthy or vigorous way
2. To make a bold or extravagant gesture or action

Hello! It's Me,

YOUR Body here.

It's Time to Listen to Me, Now.

Sally McGrath

With a new year, comes,
a new you, planning, goals and
expectations for success
in every area of your life ... right?

Your Plan for the Year Ahead

If you've set goals to improve areas of your life the five points below will set the framework to help you with your "life cleanse".

1. Reset Your Body & Mind

Scenario: You're tired of looking in the mirror seeing the same reflection that is unmotivated, not smiling back at you, and lacking the inspiration to go forward with your day. Instead you sigh and think "oh well, it is what it is" and continue on (possibly berating yourself for that extra glass of wine, not getting to sleep earlier or snoozing through the alarm).

Now it's time to create a consistent real-life routine that supports your body & mind.

2. Review Your Financial Well-being

Scenario: Agh, money! This one makes you cringe at the thought of the next credit card bill arriving in your inbox. Those "just have it" purchases during the holidays are now catching up with you and it's bringing with it heightened anxiety to the point it makes you feel physically sick. You've avoided dealing with the financial plan for the last year so now it is time to get real, it's time to bring in what you are worth! It's time to take charge and own your financial direction and planning, one-step-at-a-time.

3. Re-assess Your Career

Scenario: The thought of heading back to work fills you with dread. Do I work from home or do I go into the office? Whilst it would be great to see peers and catch up the thought of the whole day at work adds to the anxiety you are already experiencing and you wonder why you didn't put more effort into the job search last year. You've found you have a new routine that fits a daily morning routine that used to be consumed by commuting and you are more productive and the fear of this changing makes you want to change jobs. Now is the opportunity to evaluate what's working and what can be improved; job change or not.

4. Re-store Your Life

Scenario: Your life is compartmentalised, you attempt to keep work and life separate. You enjoy spending time with friends, yet often find you are comparing yourself to those around you and wishing you had made different decisions so you'd be in a different/better place now. You constantly wonder what the future will bring and planning, that's just too hard. Your life links to a cycle and the cycle for you right now is overwhelming, you know this part of your life needs attention, you just don't know where or how to start.

It's time to remove the overwhelm and create the life you really want to live, to thrive not just survive.

5. Re-evaluate Relationships

Scenario: You've got friends, family and peers in your life, maybe a partner or significant other, yet you feel dis-connected at times and would like to have deeper and more meaningful relationships. Your relationship with yourself is often a rollercoaster ride and being hard on yourself, with high expectations is normal.

It's time to find the right tribe, identify who lights you up, makes you smile and supports you (as much as you support them).

You're a hig achiever and wonder if "it's" ever going to happen!

Every year at this point in time you get to this point reflecting on what has been and where you are going and wonder what is next?

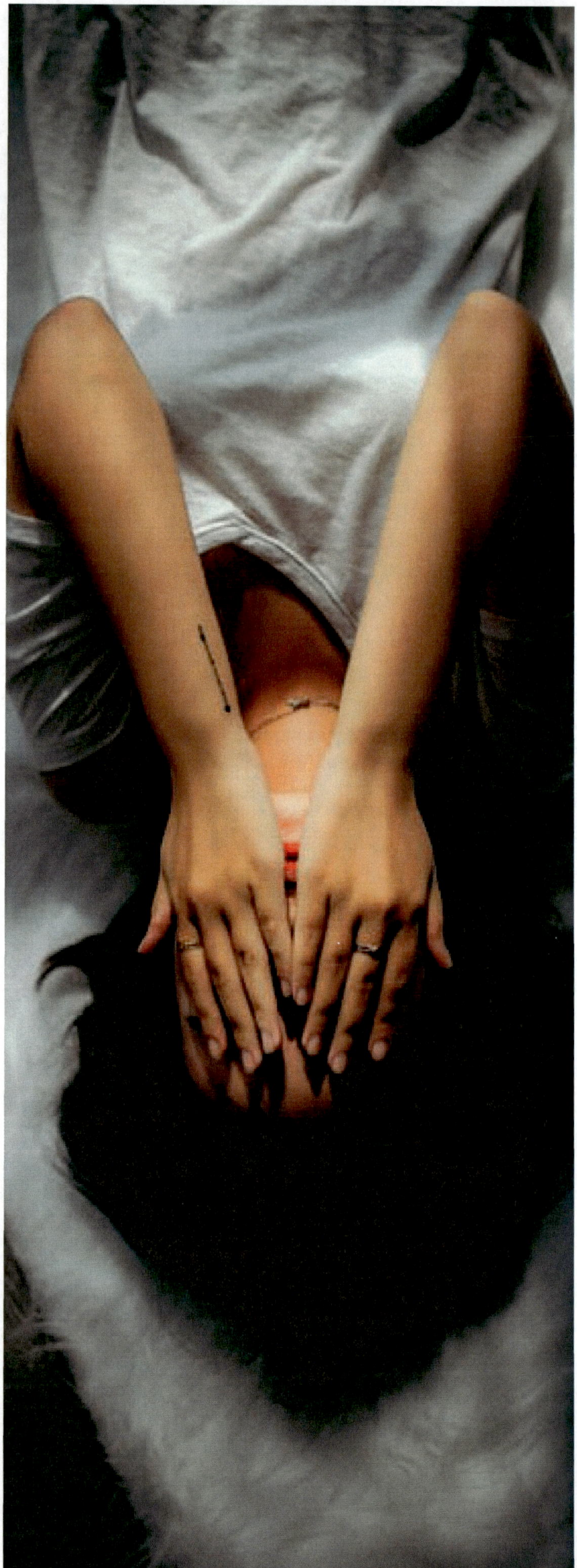

If by this point you are feeling emotionally drained, you're in the right place. It's time to "listen to your body".

We know our bodies are smart, correct? So why do we continue to ignore the signs and warnings, relentlessly pushing harder thinking we'll reach some holy grail of a "balanced life". Balance and reality are not friends. When you consider balance, think of the see-saw in the park, one side is always higher or lower than the other; and if there is balance, it's literally for a fleeting moment.

Here's my **three pillars** give you the platform to living a satisfying, fulfilling and harmonious life:

1. **Your Work & Life Synergy plan**
2. **Your Mental Hygiene plan**
3. **Your Burnout Prevention plan**

Work & Life Synergy vs Balance

If there is no balance then does that mean there is no hope? Once you identify that finding "balance and reality" don't work then you can move forward and create what is achievable and that's "work & life synergy", where you set the framework to lean in when need be, preparing and setting points to re-group and establish boundaries that will protect you and what's important to you, whilst retaining the ability to be productive and focused to deliver outcomes. Changes in the way we work and live have expedited the options to apply work and life in synergy.

Your Mental Hygiene

Mental Health has gone through a massive de-stigmatisation. Whilst some have suffered for years in silence and experiencing judgement, many have just experienced what it's like to struggle with mental health challenges, specifically what it's like to feel extreme lows where you stop caring, have zero focus and consider that opting out of life is a solution. This is why a mental hygiene plan is essential for everyone.

Considering your mental hygiene practice being similar to the exercise we do to keep our bodies fit and strong, you've got the idea behind the importance of supporting and exercising the mind in a preventative way. The combination of meditation, nutrition, stress reduction, anxiety triggers and mindset management combined with our overall outlook on life & work are contributing factors that form an integral part in developing a consistent mental hygiene plan that contributes to your preventative health and prevents the spiral into a full mental health breakdown. There is no health without mental hygiene.

How to Find THE BEST *Version of You!*

Rebecca Mcgregor

If you want to lead your best life, you need the best version of you to pursue it. The trouble is that it's all too easy to get lost along the way and put lesser versions of yourself forward.

Caroline Bellenger, award winning life coach, motivational speaker, and creator of 'Be The Impossible' started her business to take her life learning's to help others. Her journey started with the worst possible version of herself and then she discovered the best version of herself and now? She helps other people find the best in themselves too. Here are her tips for finding the best version of you.

The Five Ingredients Of The Best You

To find the best you, you need a bunch of different ingredients, but the theme of those ingredients are the same for everyone even though the precise makeup of each ingredient is totally unique for each person. You need:

1. Purpose
2. Courage
3. Self-control
4. A bit of luck
5. A lot of hard work

So, let's take a look at each of those in a bit more detail.

A Sense of Purpose

Your sense of purpose helps you to focus on the ultimate goal. It doesn't even have to be an attainable goal, just one that drives every action you take.

You simple decide what you want to be the best at. The best parent? The best employer? The best partner? The best friend? Any or all of them are fine.
Caroline's sense of purpose originated in wanting to be the best mother she could be. It meant she could no longer tolerate the destructive behaviors that had been holding her back.

But that sense of purpose expanded to include becoming the best mentor to others to help them become the best too.

A Healthy Dose Of Courage

The fear of failure can be overwhelming. Particularly, if you've had a hard time in the past. You'll see things like "the majority of businesses fail" and the self-doubt starts.

Yet, the truth is that no business succeeds without being started. No cakes get baked without breaking eggs. No houses get built without laying foundations.

The people who succeed never stop fearing failure, they just have the courage to take action anyway.

Caroline has overcome many challenges in life, but the fear they instilled isn't gone, it her courage that enables her to do things despite the fear.

Self-Control

We're not talking about control in every aspect of your life, here. We're talking about taking control of your own mind, to make it into an ally rather than an enemy.

This means facing your limiting beliefs, such as "*I can't do XYZ*" and turning them on their heads. "*Of course, I can do XYZ, Joe Bloggs came from a similar background to me, and they've done something similar, there's nothing to stop me from succeeding.*"

Caroline acknowledges that this can be a daily battle to start with, but as you progress, your confidence grows, and you see success and limiting beliefs start to dwindle away.

A Bit Of Luck

"Hey! I can't manufacture luck!"

Well, actually, you can. Research shows a peculiar thing. People who believe they are going to be lucky, are luckier than those who don't care about luck or who don't believe they're going to be lucky.

Take five minutes and write down a long list of reasons that you are lucky, right here, right now. For example, "I have a great job, beautiful kids, a nice car, etc."

And then remind yourself that you're lucky every day. Caroline says that it's her belief that she's lucky that has helped her deal with her biggest demons and achieve success.

A Lot Of Hard Work

The reason most people don't succeed is shockingly simple. They give up before they succeed.

Really. Caroline could have given up when her son was born, but it motivated her to start working to be a better person, a better parent and eventually a better mentor.

She hasn't stopped working since.

You see everyone comes across obstacles, everyone has setbacks, everyone has bad weeks or bad months, but it's those that know that and keep going, because their purpose drives them to keep going, that succeed.

Don't just work hard. Work harder than everyone around you. It's a near guarantee of success in the long-term.

Final Thoughts On Finding The Best Version Of You

Caroline took a long time to find the best version of herself. She overcame problems stemming from sexual abuse and substance abuse and she built a new life for her and her family.

Those five simple ingredients now allow her to help others do the same. If you want to be the best version of yourself, start by sorting out the basics and the rest will follow.

Be
BELLENGER
AUS

Amazing Australian Woman

Emma Gierschick OAM

Life's Backpack Full of Mystery

> "*Twenty-seven years ago I arrived in Australia for just 6 months. My backpack was full of hopes & dreams, with little room for cares or responsibilities and certainly no plans, fears or wisdom.*

I worked in cafes, bars, motels even working on a sheep station as a roustabout, hitch hiking my way around.

I thought I was exploring the world being brave and adventurous but realised 12 years later, I had actually been running away from the pain of a failed teenage marriage.

"I discovered even the world is not a big enough place to hide from yourself or your pain."

So as I pledged my allegiance of citizenship to my new homeland, I redirected my journey of travels to one of self-discovery.

I'd always been drawn to Australia, somehow learning 'Kookaburra sits in the old gum tree' at nursery and acquiring not one but 2 toy koalas. But it was the Men at Work anthem song and Waltzing Matilda that stirred something in my soul. They still do.

It's not always been easy, but it felt like I'd come home from the moment I arrived. No friends, very little money, no history or understanding of the culture, but I was determined to make it work and during the low points I reminded myself of the courage & tenacity that saw me backpack alone through Zimbabwe, on my way to Australia, stitching my own foot with my sewing kit.

I was shocked by the open racism and misogyny I witnessed when I first arrived, and probably didn't make life easy for myself by calling it out. It needed to be called out.

My life here started in Perth, flying to Sydney in time for the Mardi Gras, which was a major eye opener for this naive young woman from Yorkshire.

I had just $100 left when I decided to move on. I tossed up the idea of getting a mystery flight which cost $100 at the time, letting fate be my compass, but then decided to get the overnight coach down to Melbourne to visit the Neighbours set.

Hardly a calling from God. But the day I arrived in Melbourne I knew I was home.

I immediately began volunteer work, helping at the Positive Living Centre for people living with HIV / AIDS. So, my first real friends were primarily gay men and members of the LGTBI+ community.

Trying to fit in and feeling Melbourne was hip and cosmopolitan I commented to one of my new friends how great it was to see everyone formally recognised in society. They looked at me bewildered as I explained the 4th image on the Neighbourhood watch sign – the one of the police officer – in my mind I saw it representing the peaked cap of the gay Leather man.

My passion from childhood was natural therapies especially Reflexology and I couldn't believe my luck to see it was a recognised industry. I quickly enrolled in a 2 yr course, joined the Reflexology Association of Australia - and immediately volunteered my time.

By the AGM I put my hand up to join the committee expecting to be allocated a minor role but ended up being State Vice President as that was the only vacancy. Not phased, I was there to learn and serve not knowing the State President was leaving for a 3-month International Trip the following morning. It was a steep learning curve.

Fast forward a couple of years, and I was offered my old lecturer's job, became elected the National President of the Reflexology Association and appointed an International Director representing Australia. I joined the National and International conference circuit as a keynote speaker.

Somewhere in the middle of all this I fell madly in love with my second (ex-husband). While it didn't work out we are still in close contact and have each others back.

The 2009 bushfires hit Victoria on my birthday. I instantly swung into action contacting all Natural therapy associations, & organising volunteer teams to provide seated massage or reflexology at the staging sites for the CFA, SES etc. I simultaneously organised a national fundraising event to take place across all states providing 15 mins sessions to the public. We raised $25,000 for the Red Cross.

My father died unexpectedly a few years after and grief stricken, I felt completely lost. It was during this period that I met my daughters father taking me down a completely unexpected pathway. He was extremely violent, I thought I could 'help & fix him'. I couldn't and 4 years of extreme violence and abuse entered my life. I lost all self-confidence, became a shadow of my former self and had my baby daughter Amelia who has Down syndrome to protect.

We fled when she was 20 months old leaving with nothing. I could only afford to eat alternate days to provide for her, the Op shop became our department store. I immediately began campaigning and lobbying for greater recognition for children with a disability facing violence or abuse. I got back on the conference circuit, wrote multiple papers, cold called (and possibly stalked) a few high-ranking politicians for an opportunity to get their ear. My work in the family violence and disability fields began being recognised with awards.

I was simultaneously thrust into the start of a series of multiple legal battles with the ex. My 28th hearing over 10 years is due to take place shortly. I've won each one so far, largely self-representing by studying the law.

But there's a few more twists to our story. The year after fleeing the violence, while

in the middle of multiple legal battles, living in extreme poverty with no support I was suddenly diagnosed with breast cancer, undergoing urgent surgery, chemo and radiation therapy. I fitted my life saving treatment in around my various legal battles to protect my daughter. I was fighting a dual battle for life. For my own life physically and Amelia's legally. I then had a 'rare reaction to chemo losing use of my legs, requiring intense rehab as I learnt to walk again. I continued to campaign and lobby for children with a disability facing violence.

My work went on to be recognised with National Awards and in the 2021 Queens Birthday Honours list, **I was awarded a Medal of the Order of Australia.**

When I first received the email notifying me, I thought was either an international money scam, or my name had been mistakenly mixed up for someone else. Then when I heard there is a 2yr process involved in nominations, research and documenting evidence prior to being considered, my first thought was 'Thank god I didn't do anything too stupid in that 2 year period'

Life is good now, I'm a 7year cancer survivor, I can walk again. My daughter is a bubble of inspiration and joy, and works as a professional child model, and our legal battles are about to end – for good.

When I reflect on my arrival with just my backpack and unroll the tapestry of my life, I marvel at its colours. I can see the dark threads of pain help illuminate the colours of joy. I've realised I've succeeded when I've backed myself & that self-doubt is more challenging than any obstacle I've faced.

"I've realised I've made some 'interesting' decisions, but now with maturity - my backpack would be crammed full of wisdom, experience & the knowledge that emotional baggage is too heavy to carry - let it go."

GALE

MEET THE FUTURE YOU

READY TO LEAD? READY TO LEAD?

WWW.GALE.EDU.AU
STUDY@GALE.EDU.AU
0421 571 381

**Global Academy of
Leadership and Entrepreneurship**

Enquire about our
Leadership and Business Courses

RTO41404

Appetence
1. Desirous, wishful
2. Having or expressing desire for something

THE JOY OF REINVENTING YOUR LIFE

Words: Jean Adams

August is my birthday month and I've been thinking lately about how differently people respond to celebrating the anniversary of their birth.

For some of us, our birthday is a time when we look back over the past 12 months and pause for a while to celebrate all the things for which we are grateful.

This is a day in which we consciously choose to let our joy and exuberance shine, sometimes participating in adventurous, or ridiculously childlike activities, as we gather special people around us to celebrate having travelled another year around the sun.

Birthdays are sometimes the only time that some people pause for reflection, in their normally frantically busy lives.

Many of the female entrepreneurs in their 50s, 60s and 70s, who I work with in my capacity as Business Mentor and Empowerment Coach, admit that they have experienced a crisis of confidence when they reached significant birthday milestones of 55, 60, 65 and 70.

This is often a time when women are discovering that the life that served them well until now, no longer feels like it fits them. It feels like they have been wearing a specific type of clothing for the past 30 years that now feels like somebody else's wardrobe. These women also acknowledged that they feel as if they have become invisible and they're not sure who they are anymore.

These feelings can result in a debilitating lack of self-confidence that has sometimes led them to withdraw from the world and society in general.

In her book 'The Wisdom of Menopause' Christiane Northrup M.D. shares her personal story of how dramatically her life changed when she turned 50. Her description of what happens biologically as women reach their 50s, and their oestrogen levels drop as they journey through the different stages of menopause, means that many women feel as if the rose-tinted, oestrogen-supported glasses that they have been wearing for the past 30 years, have come off and they suddenly see the world through completely different eyes, often being shocked by the revelation of the reality in which they find themselves living. As a result, they begin to examine what is no longer working in many aspects of their lives. This leads many women to choose to reinvent the way they are living and working. Relationships that worked for them no longer bring them joy, the work they were doing feels unfulfilling and the social activities they used to enjoy, now feel like a joyless burden.

It is certainly not surprising that women facing this new reality will often leave jobs, and relationships, and move out of a home that they have been living in for many years, sometimes even moving to a new city or country to start afresh as they reinvent every aspect of their lives.
Suddenly these women find themselves joyfully independent, even though they now have to learn how to manage on their own, not only financially, but also socially. Friendships and relationships that supported them over many years during a long-term relationship may no longer be available to them. It's not surprising that many women suddenly question their self-worth and value and begin to feel invisible.
As with all life transitions, choosing to reinvent your life and adapt to a new way of living takes enormous courage and time, as you adapt physically, intellectually, spiritually, and socially to a new way of living.

The wonderful thing about being a woman in your 50s, 60s or 70s is that you have many years of experience to draw on, to inform your choices as you reinvent your life. You no longer have to apologise for being who you are. This is great news for people who have been 'people pleasers' all their lives. Walking on eggshells around people who no longer understand or encourage you to be yourself, can be exhausting! You can now bravely stand up and say, "this is who I am, I love myself enough to step into my power and shine my magnificence and I choose to surround myself with people who will authentically cheer me on as I do that." If you've spent your life apologising for who you are, then its' time to stop. It's time to step out of your comfort zone, knowing that you will have some speed wobbles, yet being brave enough to embrace who you are. As Brené Brown says, "Owning our story and loving ourselves through the process, is the bravest thing we will ever do."

It's time to stop apologising for being you. It's time to embrace your unique magnificence. It's time to create a life that brings you joy and abundance. It's time to let go of everything that no longer serves you. It's time to let go of all the habits, possessions, relationships, and activities that weigh you down, wear you out and make you feel like a shadow of who you truly are. You might be thinking that reinventing yourself feels daunting. Yet, if you look at all the positive, mature women who we consider to be courageous role models, they all started exactly where you are right now. Imagine what would happen if you chose to have the courage to embrace all your beautiful inner wildness, quirkiness, and differences, and share them with the world. You would feel optimistic every day because you are living your truth!

Age is only a number, and if you choose not to let it define you, then you will soar!

There are always role models to guide you, as you step courageously into your unique magnificence. Amazing women such as Iris Apfel, who at 100 years of age is still a fashion icon. Ita Buttrose, at 80 years of age, is proudly active in her role as Chair of the Australian Broadcasting Corporation. Jane Fonda is still acting at 84 years of age. Numerous other mature women will inspire you to step into your mature, feminine power. Women such as Oprah Winfrey, (68 years), Michelle Obama (58 years), Jamie Lee-Curtis (63 years), and Ruth Bader-Ginsberg, who was still working as an Associate Justice of the Supreme Court of the United States, when she died in 2020 at 87 years of age.

Yes, it may feel daunting to step out of the life you have been living. Yes, you will need support, even before you take the first steps. Always remember that you are never alone. Reach out and ask for help from someone that you trust to guide you be impartial as they walk beside you and help you on the next steps of your journey. Find a mentor, a counsellor, or someone impartial to help you. Someone who has experienced managing life and career transitions themselves. However well-meaning family and close friends may be, they often won't understand what you need as you step into your new way of living. Some of them may find your courage challenges their perceptions of how life is meant to be lived as well!

Think instead of what you want every aspect of your life to look like, on your next birthday. Where do you want to be living? Who do you want around you? What work are you doing? How are you filling your life with joy, love, happiness, hope, faith, and courage? When you think of yourself sitting in your rocking chair at 95 years of age, what do you want your memories to look like?

Choose to courageously step out of your comfort zone, starting today. Take one step at a time, one day at a time.

As George Eliot (the pen name used by Mary Ann Evans) said:

"It's never too late to be what you might have been"

Meet Jean Adams

Jean is a Business Mentor and Empowerment Coach. She is obsessed with empowering female entrepreneurs in their 50s, 60s and 70s to gain the clarity and confidence to enable them to elevate their business growth and achieve their dreams and goals.

She mentors women who have an existing business, as well as women who are creating a new business so that they can leverage out of working in full-time employment into working for themselves.

Jean works with her clients to help them create a solid foundation of systems, strategies, tools and processes to amplify their business growth and personal productivity.

Drawing on her 30+ years of experience and expertise in corporate leadership, sales, marketing, administration, and event management, Jean helps her clients identify their target market, clarify their business message, create simple lead generation, sales and marketing systems, as well as guiding them on how to find the best networks to support them on their journey.

It's Always About Community

Hepburn in Conversation with - Lauren Sherson

When Hepburn started in 2020 we were privileged to speak with Liberal party candidate Lauren Sherson. Now two years on we invited Lauren Sherson back to speak with us again to find out what has happened over the last couple of years. Lauren talks about her Drive-in Gigs concept, her love for her community, and her reasons for entering into politics.

Indeed, it has certainly been an action packed couple of years. Even despite the lockdowns we've had here in Victoria. Like many people in Victoria and around Australia, I had to change what I was doing so that I could continue, and particularly with entrepreneurship education, which has been my career for almost 20 years.

My career in entrepreneurship education provided the diversity in the people as well as a diversity in the ventures and the concepts that come I saw. This experience really prepares you for everything. It is just constantly interesting. I'm so fascinated in the human mind and human behaviour. I ended up going back to Melbourne University and doing psychological research.

And when you're looking at entrepreneurship and the theory of it, from the human aspect, the psychological aspect of entrepreneurship comes down to one's personal commitment toward an opportunity. When you have that understanding and looking at that type of behaviour, it teaches you how to motivate other people, how to bring teams together, how to raise communities to make impact and change in the world.

I'm an ideas person. Lockdowns are not going to lockdown your ideas. And I remember when the Grand Prix was cancelled after the gates had opened and people had already arrived, I'm thought about how safe it is for people to be in their car and the concept of Drive-in Gigs and state in which would enable people to have a rock concert from their car emerged. Drive-in Gigs was a way to bring joy and optimism back into Victoria and support the music industry.

Frustratingly, the state government would not allow the team to proceed with that idea as we would be congregating people, which was against the pandemic laws. And so that initiative ended up being more of a campaign about how do we get Aussies to get paid gigs? And while that was really relevant during COVID, it's still relevant now.

We still have a scenario where artists are struggling to put food on their table and to pay for electricity and the smaller venues are struggling to find a way to be able to pay live music performers to play in their venues.

Drive-in Gigs received so much support. And there was even a local petition that had just under a thousand signatures. And when I'm down in St Kilda now people still bring Drive-in Gigs up in conversation or talk about it. And so while the venture itself never really got up, and we didn't hold a concert, the concept of it has really stayed with people and has become a symbol of how we were fighting for artists during COVID.

I am so passionate about how, what inspires a community can be used to create new government policy and new initiatives to help increase our quality of life.

In my twenties I was one of the start-up people who was out there to revolutionize the world. It got to a point where I realized there is so many barriers to growth that it really required for me to be in the room where legislation can be made or changed, where advocacy can have real impact, rather than just be noise out on the street.

During 2020, I was focused on local government initiatives and I was put on the ticket. But because of the lockdowns, we weren't allowed to campaign out on the street. We weren't allowed to do letterbox dropping, we weren't allowed to go to meetings. So all we could do was digital and focus on blocks of voters and how to get community leaders engaged so that in turn, their communities would be engaged with what we're doing.

And what I loved about that local aspect in 2020 is that it was so on the ground and here in Melbourne there was that appetite for mental health, which really was about healthy minds. Healthy Business was my tagline back then. And the mental health initiatives needed to be human to human and face to face, and that had been taken away from us the people. And as we know now, had severe detrimental consequences.

And if we fast forward two years, it's about recovery, our quality of life, our liveability, our relationships and what we choose to do.
I learned many years ago with my passion in entrepreneurship and in mental health or psychology that the greatest political impact that I could have is at a state level. And I've had amazing mentors with current and former members of Parliament. And the way it was explained to me is that at a state level, I can advocate and get initiatives up and running that can then be rolled out nationally and then be adopted and rolled out internationally by other countries. Whereas when you run for a federal seat, it can be so difficult, to be way down here in Melbourne. The people's needs and their wants are so different across the country.

So state level politics enables us to have a greater impact and a faster impact. But it also means I get to come home and sleep in my own bed and see my husband and dog every day. I have no desire to be on a plane every week. I did that in my twenties. I was flying interstate or overseas every week for nearly ten years. I got that out of my system. I am now where my heart and my soul is.

I need to be here in Melbourne and be near our community members. It defeats the purpose, if I'm spending 26 weeks a year in Canberra, I'd rather be here and hearing people and attending the events and building all the advocacy and the new policy and the initiatives and introducing people to create better private enterprise initiatives.

Entering into politics is the greatest and most humble thing one can do. It is to serve as a politician for the people. I recently had a meeting with a local primary school that's looking at issues of safety around their school grounds. They have asked me to articulate what

their challenges are and to convey that need, to advocate on their behalf. I'm excited to be able to advocate when people say they need this to be funded or this policy to be up in this area, and to help the people in my community.

I find rather than being noise in the background, I look to be in a position where my entrepreneurship training, problem selection and really seeking ways to get things up and happening comes into play. It takes a community to raise an opportunity or a venture. And I like being part of that community. It's not about me being the champion.

I really love reading the philosophies of Lao Tsu and his definition of good leadership: 'A leader is best when people barely know he exists, when his work is done, his aim fulfilled, they will say: we did it ourselves'.

There are leaders who want all of the acknowledgment and praise but the best leaders support their people. And so for me, being a politician is about how do we support champions in their cause? It's their issues, their communities. And they have opened the doors and welcomed me and shared their challenges.

And being in the Liberal Party, it's fundamental for us or for government to get out of the way and so I'm able to go in and find out the problem and trigger or catalyse and advocate and make the change happen and then step back and again. I want to find the real champions and watch them in their success and see the flow on effect that their cause has in their community.

It is inspiring and humbling.

Having taught entrepreneurship and having been an academic researcher, I have a strong understanding of entrepreneurship. I find the idea of entrepreneurship gets so diluted today and people associate entrepreneurship with business. And when I say it's not, people look at me a little bit strangely.

Of course, you can be an entrepreneurial business owner, but not all businesses are entrepreneurial. So for me, looking at the science of entrepreneurship and the academic side of it, it's about creating something that's new and useful for others in its most simple form.

It's very much about how do we get new thinking, how do we find a new perspective? And from that new way of looking at something, what new thing can we create? Or is there something that we've forgotten about and cast aside at the time, for whatever reason, that we need to go back to. I believe unless your eyes are wide open, judgment and bias creeps in.

I find it so interesting when I'm out in community and I'm chatting with people. It takes me back to the many years in education, the thousands of entrepreneurship students and taking them from ideation, when they've got that first epiphany through to helping them reshape their idea and getting them to pitch to external stakeholders and early stage investors or government departments, large corporations or even local community groups.

And going through that process, I'm finding when I'm out in community now, it feels as though I'm back in that entrepreneurship education phase because I'm following people's thinking and there is no judgment. It's not about me having an emotional attachment. I suddenly have compassion and a lot of compassion for them. But it means that I'm able to identify and articulate the essence and the core aspects which need to be focused upon in order to make the greatest amount of progress possible.

When I ask people how they ended up in the room today, whether they are a guest speaker or I'm sitting down face to face with an individual, nearly every person responds with an initial bit of a chuckle, and saying that they never imagined or expected that they'd be in this career, this job, this position, this venture. And that reflects life.

It's not a ladder that you're climbing. It's being responsive rather than reactive to the opportunities that are around you. And it might sound cliché to follow your heart and your passion, but it is a good place to start and then start looking for those opportunities.

During COVID people had time to themselves and once they got over it or they binge watched all they could do, they started creating; getting into writing or painting or sewing, or maybe it was woodwork, or maybe it wasn't even art related at all. And people found new passions and new purposes.

I believe if you are starting out on an entrepreneurial journey, you need to find yourself mentors and peers to talk with. It comes back to community every single time. Immerse yourself in a community of people that do what you love doing. And from that place, that's when opportunities will open up. That's when you'll have the support to be in a position, to be able to see the opportunities that are there and to fight for those opportunities.

You really have to fight like hell if you want to succeed, if there's something you want. So without the personal commitment, it won't work. So if you know the commitment is not there, then move on.

One of the things I learnt in entrepreneurship was to 'give it 48'. If you haven't started within 48 hours, your heart's not in it and move on to the next thing. And I wholeheartedly believe in that.

This interview with Lauren Sherson can be heard on the Hepburn in Conversation podcast.

Amazing Australian Women
Dr Red Ruby Scarlet

Words: Georgie Arnaud

Dr Red Ruby Scarlet is creative, passionate, outspoken and undeniably, a powerful and Amazing Australian Woman.

Dr Red is an activist, early childhood teacher-researcher, consultant, speaker, artist and academic with 30 years of experience in early education. She is an advocate for healthy, supportive early education environments and promoting a universal respect for social justice and Aboriginal cultures. Her drive and willingness to defy the norm both in education and the artistic world, is influential to the new generation of creative industries and the future of educational practice.

Dr Scarlet knew that she was destined for a career in early education from the beginning of her higher studies. She completed her Bachelor of Education (Early childhood Education and Teaching) with first class honours at The University of Western Sydney in 2004. She then went on to complete her Doctor of Philosophy (PhD) in Early Childhood Education in 2010 at the University of Melbourne.

After her studies she quickly became a Postdoctoral Research Fellow at the Childhood Research Collective University of Canberra where she began cultivating her expertise and interest in early childhood education further. She held this position for two years before becoming an Artist In Residence at the London Metropolitan University in 2013. Here she was able to broaden her insight into education and the value of art even more so, and under a different cultural context. Based on her expertise in these areas, she was selected to be a contributor to the Australian early childhood national curriculum and national quality framework. She has also written for Play School - the much loved Australian children's television show.

A year into her residence she became Creative Director of MultiVerse, an organisation dedicated to providing resources and support to the education and community sectors, in which she still currently contributes her educational advice and knowledge. Through this role she aims to promote inclusivity of practises including within high quality

art opportunities and endorses the vitality of creativity not just within our everyday lives but in the work force also.

Dr Scarlet additionally teaches part-time in Sydney at Clovelly Children's Centre. On top of these positions, she manages to fit in a leadership role in the Social Justice in Early Childhood group as well. Red is the founder of the Social Justice in Early Childhood Foundation.

In 2017, Dr Scarlet called for critical though into whether days like Father's Day, Mother's Day and all akin cultural celebrations were considered necessary educational content as part of curriculum when they inherently generalise and therefore exclude, striking major attention from the media. She went on 'Today Tonight' explaining that questioning such events would allow people in diverse family situations and who identify to feel included in various celebrations and encourage a warm sense of community. In light of children's rights and developing their sense of belonging,

Dr Scarlet believes rethinking celebrations in education would be beneficial and wasn't afraid to have her opinion heard. Her bravery when speaking out about a controversial and long instated tradition is immensely inspiring to those feeling silenced by normalised societal structures such as Father's Day and Mother's Day. Dr Scarlet's ongoing influence is empowering to others who wish to speak their mind even if it may ruffle some feathers at first.

The importance of artistic expression within early childhood is often overlooked however, Red has been instrumental in promoting an awareness of the perception associated with art and how this should be re-evaluated. The arts are an outlet to freely explore emotion and are essential to the healthy functioning of the business world, yet it seems a negative stigma has come into place in relation to the creative industries and how essential they really are. Dr Scarlet is working to abolish this stigma and grow the incorporation of art in educational practices, specifically within early childhood.

Through her creation of the 'Inclusion Room' Dr Scarlet has provided a space for educators to become more inclusive with their practises by educating themselves on Aboriginal cultures and how to cater to a diverse range of students in different circumstances. This, along with many other projects Red has up and running, is implementing a new future in quality education.

"My mumma voted in the 67 referendum but Aboriginal people's lives should never be the result of a public vote on their own country."

- @RedRubyScarlet

Dr Scarlet has delivered numerous powerfully influential keynote speeches expressing her views on the education space and has also completed multiple published works detailing the importance of engaging in art during youth. She has co-written and stars in a musical about early childhood education and art entitled 'The National Quality Framework – The Musical!'. She is a trailblazer for inclusivity and creative expression in education and a leader to those entering the profession or equally as engulfed by artistry.

Abundance

1. The state or condition of having a copious quantity of something; plentifulness

2. Plentifulness of the good things of life; prosperity

"if not me,
who?
If not now,
when?"

Emma Watson

"The only thing
standing between
where you are now &
vhere you want to be, is
your thinking."

Oxygen or Sales
The Business Dilemma

Words: Julia Zielke

"This may sound a little dramatic BUT sales are literally the oxygen of business. And if sales are the oxygen, customers are the life blood."

My purpose and my absolute passion in life is to empower you with the mindset and the sales strategies to do more of what you love AND make a great profit. I know when you do what you LOVE you will make a difference in the lives of those around you. Imagine if together we could inspire others to discover and do what they love every day? Call me a dreamer but that sounds like an awesome world for my children to grow up in!

But how can you do what you LOVE, if you don't know how to sell? As a business owner, if you don't make a great profit how will your business survive, or even better, be wildly successful? How will you land your dream job if you can't sell yourself.

For the last 20 years, sales have been my life. After finishing a Business Marketing and a Sport Science degree I begrudgingly fell into a Sales role. As an introvert and a Marketing major, I thought that 'sales' was beneath me and way too scary! But the lure of international travel in my first sales role was too strong to turn down. And here I am 20 years later.

As a Professional Sales Representative I have sold everything from knock down furniture (think IKEA style) into major retails chains in Australia, to gym memberships, to advertising space in a National Newspaper and prescription medication. I learnt to LOVE selling

I didn't love selling for the dollars, the rewards, the fancy hotels, or incredible conference venues (which were all amazing), I loved the people and the connections and knowing that my product or service made a difference in the lives of others. Even the furniture made a difference, by making life easier and more affordable for thousand of people.

So, let me ask you this, do you LOVE what you do? Does your product or service or job make a difference in the life of someone else? If you answered YES!

Then I can help you to LOVE selling too.

LIFE IS TOO SHORT

Here's the reason why I think we all need to be courageous and start doing what we love today!

I remember lying, buried in freezing cold snow. I was 13. I couldn't move my arms or my legs. I could barely scream from the weight of the snow on my chest. I tried thrashing around, but it was no use. It could see nothing but darkness. The only thing I could do was use the heat of my breath to make a cocoon around my mouth so I could breathe.

I didn't know it at the time but I had fallen into a creek and had been avalanched by snow.

I learnt to ski when I was 3, so skiing 'off piste' (outside the designated ski runs) was not uncommon. There had been a huge 'dump' of snow the night before. This is every skier's dream, lots of snow and fresh tracks. The problem is, with so much snow it often covers up otherwise obvious obstacles, like creeks and large rocks.

The snow had created a loose bridge over a creek. As Mum, who was skiing in front of me, skied over the bridge it loosened the snow then as I followed her, it collapsed.

I fell headfirst into the creek and was buried by the surrounding snow. Thankfully the creek was shallow enough that I wasn't completely immersed in water.

Mum saved my life that day. Her 'Motherly Instinct' kicked in. She trudged herself 50 meters back up the steep hill, in knee deep snow to try to find me. All she could see was a sea of white. With no sign of me, she somehow knew where to start digging. After 20 minutes of digging with her bare hands, she pulled me out of the hole that was as deep as her shoulders.

I was completely fine. I had hypothermia and I was a little shaken. But I was alive.

I don't remember us talking about the incident much as a family and I was back out skiing a few days later. But something in that moment stuck with me.

It made me realize that life could be VERY short.

Two decades later the impact of my skiing accident really hit home for me. I discovered what I REALLY LOVE doing, but I wasn't doing it.

Knowing that life could be VERY short was the driving force behind my decision to leave my full time, secure job during Covid and start my business as a Sales and Mindset Coach.

What would you do if you knew that you could make millions from it and you knew that people needed it?

FIND YOUR PURPOSE

This was and always will be my #1 tool to sell yourself, your product or your service.

What do you LOVE doing? That one thing that you could do all day and you could do it for free. You thought about it when you answered my question above. WHY do you love it so much? How does it make you feel?

In that thought lies your passion and your purpose. Our purpose is a combination of our unique gift to the world and the impact that gift has on others.

If you can easily think of that 'thing', I want you to know how fortunate you are. If you are already doing what you LOVE every day, you should feel so proud of your courage to pursue it.

If you area anything like me 8 years ago and have no idea, you are not alone.

Feeling flat and un-inspired 8 years ago I came across Simon Sinek's work. I was in yet another sales training session, working in the Pharmaceutical industry and I was un-inspired. Until the trainer went 'off script' and showed us Simon Sinek's TED talk - How Great Leaders Inspire Action.

It fundamentally changed my life.

Simon changed the way I sell, the way I communicate, and most importantly the way I show up in the world.

He taught me how to find my purpose. And how to communicate from a place of purpose rather than continually seeking a result.

He taught me that the point of business and life is not to work with everyone or be friends with everyone. It's to connect with people who believe what you believe. People who 'get you' and align with your WHY (your purpose).

Simon's theory didn't just appeal to me on an emotional level, there is science behind it. Boom my rational brain was engaged.

Simon teaches us that the part of our brain that makes decisions is called the Limbic brain. The Limbic brain has no capacity for language, only emotion. So, if we want people to buy from us, to like us or to listen to us we MUST connect on that emotional level first so they can make a decision.

I can almost guarantee that you would have a selection of products and services that you buy, and you are loyal to, not because they are cheap or because they have the best features but because of the way they make you feel. Apple is a prime example; they are certainly not the cheapest and often don't have the best features and yet people would line up for hours to be the first to have a new device. It's because of the way they make us feel. Cool, connected, different, better than, trusted. Which ever emotion Apple evokes for you is why you keep going back (or not going there at all).

Simon coined the phrase "START WITH WHY".

When we start our marketing messages and our sales calls from our purpose, our WHY we are allowing people to decide if they 'get us', if the like us. And for my fellow 'people pleasers', the sooner we learn that it's ok for people not to like us, the sooner we find those who do.

This has become the #1 sales and communication tool that I teach and that I use in my business. If you haven't already, go and watch Simon Sinek's TED talk - How Great Leaders Inspire Action and discover your WHY.

How to Succeed in the Cryptocurrency Industry

Starting with a Growth Mindset

Alice Huang

Much like other industries, cryptocurrency and blockchain projects can have the same issues with scalability, productivity. and efficiency. Here, I outline the steps, I took to help my growth trajectory in the recent years to pivot from the very traditional real estate industry, into the world of cryptocurrency.

Be warned, crypto never sleeps!

Background

I have 15 years of corporate real estate consulting experience, and used my property knowledge to launch a boutique real estate development firm in Texas which I currently own and manage with my business partner. Being passionate about cryptocurrency, I began consulting on cryptocurrency projects as an Interim Chief Operations Office (COO) in 2021. I've been working on various projects; some for Initial Coin Offering (ICO) and some for Initial Public Offering (IPO).

My job is to stay agile and open minded. I learn about the project first, and then determine the goals that need to be set. I can then clearly see the gaps that need to be filled.

I've been consulting on business operations for several years now, with the most recent operations consulting clients being in SaaS and digital marketing; it was somewhat of a natural progression to move into Web3.

Although I have a Diploma of Technology, the technology I learned back in 2006, is now obsolete. I needed to take the time to learn what cryptocurrency was, and why the technology behind cryptocurrency was important. I can comfortably now say that I have solid knowledge in this field.

If you want to succeed in the cryptocurrency scene but do not have a strong technical background, dont fret. You can still add value to the industry.

"Developing a growth mindset is the key to succeed in any personal or professional project."

Develop a Growth Mindset

I am a very different person now than I was 15 years ago. In my teens and early 20's, I was comfortable, living in Vancouver, Canada and never wanted to leave my hometown. I didn't know who I was and I didn't know what I wanted in life.

What changed? I went from having a fixed mindset to a growth mindset. I've built up an intense sense of curiosity; this allows me to adapt quickly by remaining open minded. It all started when I lived overseas for the first time in my life in 2009. It was eye opening! I had a good ten years of personal growth in one year.

A book that I highly recommend and that was instrumental in changing my approach to life: Mindset: The New Psychology of Success by Carol S. Dweck. The book confirms that anyone can develop a growth mindset, at any stage of life.

You can take the process as slow as you need. It's best to try something new every day. It doesn't have to be big, but it is important to pick something that challenges you. It can just be learning a phrase in Spanish and using it when you are traveling, or trying out a new dish that you would never otherwise try.

Another method that I found worked really well for me, especially during the pandemic lockdowns, is listening to podcasts and audiobooks. I've listened to over 2,000 podcasts and audiobooks since 2020. These resources have helped tremendously with my personal and professional growth. These inspirational podcasts by successful entrepreneurs, respected scientists, and life-changing psychologists are pivotal to my transition, personal and professional growth.

I am sure you have heard this saying "you are the average of the five people you spend the most time with" by Jim Rohn. By listening to these podcasts, I was surrounded by people I normally wouldn't have been exposed to.

Developing a growth mindset is the key to succeed in any personal or professional project. I went from someone who never wanted to leave the city I grew up in, to someone who has lived in eight countries across four continents with ease. I am now driven by curiosity and personal growth.

Once I understood that anyone can develop a growth mindset and that anyone can learn and grow at any age, then pivoting into new industries becomes much easier. It feels like I had escaped the Matrix when that clicked for me.

It's All About Networking

I am sure you've all heard this before...it's not what you know, it's who you know. I tend to find that to be true in the crypto world as well. Nowadays, most of my clients come from referrals. I am also introducing clients to those I've worked with on previous projects as well.

Take action! Join your local meetups and start networking. You never know who could be looking for the talent that you have!

Cryptocurrency/Web3 Project Challenges

There are, much like traditional industries, many challenges in the cryptocurrency space. One of the main difficulties is that it is so new and unregulated. This can be seen as a pro and a con.

The pro is that anyone with an idea can have a chance to get involved as an early insert, but since it is not tightly regulated, it can sometimes feel like the Wild West; that the standards in the market can be lower than industries that are strictly regulated. Some of the projects are not properly managed, they have no real tokenomics behind the projects. Their main goal is to "make money". Making money is definitely a great objective to have, especially for investors, but the project needs to have a solid foundation and a team that cares.

Unfortunately, during my early days as a crypto COO, I was involved with an accidental rug-pull project. Rug-pull meaning that the core team lacks the intention of delivering the promised project. Accidental rug-pull meaning that the team has no ability to deliver. I left the organization soon after learning the core team had no real goals and visions for the project, except to make the coin worth a dollar.

How were they going to achieve this? By using hype! Projects are bound to fail if they are based solely on hype and have no actual usage or a market-need for the project. I was able to increase our project value by 16x within 5 hours of launch, but it soon came crashing down due to the lack of real tokenomics.

To stand out in the industry, you need to bring a strong business acumen to the industry, even if it's not directly related to technology. Any previous business experiences can be valuable. The majority of those in the industry have a strong technical background but not necessarily good management skills; as such, these projects need specialists who can manage multiple projects, meet deadlines, represent the projects in public and build partnerships with other meaningful projects.

Another important lesson I learned from this project is that it has the same issues as any other companies, such as:

- inability to scale due to the lack of systems and processes;
- A lack of shared visions and goals among the team members, especially senior staff;
- inability in managing multiple projects and deadlines;
- unable to correctly forecast the demand and use for a product;
- lack of go-to-market strategies;
- poor planning of resources; and
- internal disagreements.

Alice Huang

As a consulting COO, my job is to learn the project as soon as possible. Once I know the project well enough, then I find out what is the ultimate goal for the project. It is my job to figure out where the gaps are so I can close those gaps from where we are to where we want to be.

Alice grew up in Vancouver, Canada and spent 2011 to 2016 living in Melbourne, Australia. She has extensive experience in real estate consultancy, operations, marketing and sales. She has been able to adapt easily to living in eight countries in her adult life due to her adventurous and open spirit. She now resides in Montreal, Canada.

Her career path has been diverse. She's taught art classes to children and English to adults in Canada and China. She has also worked her way up from being an Executive Assistant to a COO, to being a COO herself. She's worked in the restaurant and hotel industry in Australia and Canada. She also founded and sold a property management company in Taiwan.

Alice has worked for PropTech and HealthTech startups in the UK. She started a women's self defense retreat in Germany. She then moved to Mexico City to learn Spanish in 2019 and that's when she discovered remote consulting work. After Mexico City, Alice moved to Texas and co-founded a boutique real estate development company which currently has a team of 10 employees. She manages the company remotely from Canada.

She has now launched a crypto consulting business on helping launch blockchain projects.

Amazing Australian Women Phoebe Dray

Words: Rebecca Mcgregor

Financial literacy: the missing piece of the puzzle in the fight for gender equality

As the founder of Phoebe Dray Consultancy (PDC), I provide innovative business consulting, group coaching, keynote speaking and business workshops, as I believe small businesses need guidance to ensure longevity and success.

Recently, it occurred to me how much family life can play a role in the way I service my clients. When my dad was unwell recently, despite it being nothing life-threatening, it put my mum in a tailspin. For all the reasons you would expect, however one of them really highlighted to me the absolute importance of being financially literate.

Mum was in a panic as she isn't clear on where all of their finances are at. Where the bills are paid, how the bills are paid, how to access their different bank accounts, what shares they own and the list goes on. It was concerning to see my mum paralysed by this uncertainty, overwhelmed, and frightened about what would happen to her if my father was to pass away.

This brought home to me just how important it is for every female, young, old and in-between to understand their finances, personal and business. To be "Financial Literate" and in control of their own financial future.

How can you become financially literate and have confidence in taking control of your money?

1. Become Accountable

Don't just let your partner, bookkeeper or accountant do the finances for you. My number one saying is "Never abdicate, always delegate". By this, I mean that it is important for you to understand your numbers, understand your financial reports, where your money is going and how you pay your bills. Even if you aren't doing the processing and administration yourself, it is key that you do know what is happening, you take an interest in the finance side of your life and can confidently take charge if you need to.

2. Ask questions

If you are not sure about something, ask questions. Whether it is of your partner, your accountant or bookkeeper or other trusted advisor, ask questions. I am of the belief that there is no question too silly, especially when it comes to your finances, the more questions you ask and the greater understanding you get, the more confident you will become.

3. Review Your position regularly

Take time every month to review your reports and financial position. I personally use Xero for both my business and my personal finances.

I love to review my reports regularly and if I am not sure of anything I can easily take a deeper look into the numbers or seek guidance from someone. Doing this will assist you in really understanding how you are spending your money and making sure that there is no money leaking out of your business or personal financial position.

Having confidence in the financial aspect of your personal life and business is the key to your secure financial future. If you are not sure and need more assistance seek help to build your knowledge and confidence.

> *"Never abdicate, always delegate"*

MAKING YOUR NEXT MOVE?

READY TO LEAD? READY TO LEAD?

WWW.GALE.EDU.AU
STUDY@GALE.EDU.AU
0421 571 381

GALE

Global Academy of Leadership and Entrepreneurship

Enquire about our
Leadership and Business Courses

RTO41404

Ambition
1. An earnest desire and determination to achieve success.

Imposter Syndrome
What is it & Why should we care

Words: Rachel Lounds

There's a lot of buzz around this topic at the moment, from it being covered in multiple business articles, mentioned in passing to medical students in training or openly advertised on internal job boards.

But what exactly is imposter syndrome and why should you care?

Let's start by making sure we are completely clear on what imposter syndrome is NOT.

It is not, nor has it ever been a diagnosable psychological disorder of any kind. You are not broken, you do not need medication to fix you and in fact as you will find out shortly, there are perfectly good reasons why you may feel like an imposter.

It is also not a fancy term for self-esteem, think of self-esteem as a kind of global sense that we have of ourselves. Imposter syndrome is specific to achievement arenas like career, business or performance of any kind.

It's unlikely you will feel like an imposter doing the laundry or going grocery shopping but you might if you are going for a job interview or about to give a big presentation.

The word 'syndrome' therefore is a tad misleading. The original term, imposter phenomenon, was first coined in 1978 in a study by two psychologists, Dr. Pauline Clance and Dr. Suzanne Imes, that has since been replicated in multiple other studies with similar findings, revealing that millions of people globally from CEO's to doctors, students, lawyers and corporate employees, secretly believe that they are not as smart, talented, skilled, intelligent or knowledgeable as other people seem to think that they are.

And the most surprising thing about imposter syndrome is that people feel like this despite sometimes overwhelming and compelling evidence of their success.

So What's Going On?

People who experience imposter feelings often externalise their success to outside factors like luck, timing, help from others or that people 'were just being nice'.

They explain their success and accomplishments not as something they can do or have done but as a result of external factors. So, as a result, each time they accomplish something it is emotionally unclear for them how they got there, which means the only possible explanation is that they have fooled people. And if you think you have been fooling others all this time your biggest fear is going to be being found out or exposed.

Core Reasons

The topic of imposter syndrome has somewhat been over psychologised, meaning it is most often referred to in individual terms, and that there is something inherently wrong with us that we must fix. However, there are multiple reasons why you may experience imposter syndrome and it's important to understand them so you can contextualise more and personalise less.

Family dynamics

Our parents did their best to raise us but sometimes they inadvertently pass on messages or expectations that may lead to us feeling like an imposter later in life.

Perhaps you had parents who rarely praised you for your accomplishments and were quick to point out your failures?

Maybe your parents compared you to other siblings or children making you feel like you didn't measure up?

Maybe they had expectations of you going to college, the military, the family business or to produce grandchildren?

Whatever it may be, they were trying to do their best, but those unintentional messages from our families became internalized over time. So, it is useful here to understand how your successes and failures were reacted to and perceived by your family in you developing those feelings of being an imposter.

But we weren't all raised by the same people and so there is more to it than that.

The Confidence Gap

One of the contributing factors to imposter feelings is the well documented confidence gap between people who identify as women and people who identify as men. A recent study done by Zenger Folkman of 10,000 people (half of whom were outside of the US) found that confidence is lowest in women in their 20s, rises slightly in their 30s, starts to even out around mid 40's and 50s and by 60, women are more confident than men. That is a very long time to wait to feel confident when considering your 20s and 30s are key career platform building years. This also has a very clear and significant financial impact on retirement for women.

One of a few or the only

You may be one of the few or the only person who looks or sounds like you in your company or field. Specific areas where women, people of colour or people who have a disability may not be found such as engineering, politics and C-suite positions can lead people to feeling like they are an imposter purely because a sense of belonging fosters confidence and if you do look and sound differently to the majority of those around you, you may feel like you don't belong.

Situational Factors

If you work alone or are a solopreneur/self employed you are also more prone to imposter syndrome, mainly because you have no one to bounce ideas off and are essentially doing your own performance evaluation, making you more likely to judge yourself more harshly.

Also, with a lot of people now working remotely due to the pandemic, there is an increase in imposter feelings being felt across the board because of this disconnectedness from others.

Other situations where you may experience these feelings are if you work in a creative field. Often in these fields everything you do is up for scrutiny professionally and publicly. There are numerous examples of famous people who admit to feeling imposter syndrome fro Michelle Pfeifer to Tom Hanks, from Maya Angelou to Tina Fey.

It is also common for people who work in rapidly changing, information dense fields like medicine, engineering, or science and technology, to feel this way. All the fields where no human could possibly keep up, yet many feel that they 'should', and in highly competitive fields like law and medicine where people are literally vying for the next position up.

These are just some of the factors that may contribute to why you may feel like an imposter.

For more information on other contributing factors and identifying your personal patterns, I suggest connecting with me about the Rethinking Imposter SyndromeT™ program and we can discuss ways to help you overcome some of those challenges

The impact on your career

Imposter syndrome feelings lead to behaviours and those behaviours have consequences. Pauline Clance and Suzanne Imes identified coping strategies that people who experience imposter syndrome commonly use to manage the anxiety of being found out and to avoid being found out.

Flying under the radar - Holding back in your career and not putting yourself forward for projects or promotions. The thinking here is that 'if I stay low then no one will notice I don't really know what I am doing.'

Procrastination - I think we all know this one! We are hardwired to avoid things we don't like but this becomes a problem when it affects our ability to carry out our work tasks, business objectives or career and life goals. The thinking here is that if you didn't really try then you have an excuse for why you failed, but if you do succeed, you can still blame it on fooling them again, right?

Self-sabotage - You may unconsciously sabotage your success by turning up late, forgetting things, purposefully not really trying or perhaps even having a few too many drinks the night before a big presentation or a job interview. The thinking here is that if I try and fail people will 'know' I am stupid, so I'd rather they think I am lazy and unmotivated.

It's useful to understand which strategy you tend to use so you can become more aware of how imposter syndrome is impacting your career progress and potential.

The 'cure'

The only way to stop feeling like an imposter is to stop thinking like an imposter. How do we do that?

Well, we need to contextualise it to understand the core reasons we may feel it. Then look at how we can reframe our thinking and develop some self-compassion.

Instead of thinking:

"I have no idea what I am doing", try thinking "I may not know everything I need to know right now but I am smart enough to find out".

It may not be easy but talking about these nebulous feelings of self doubt is a great place to start, with 70% of people experiencing it, you are not alone. However, I want to caution not to get stuck here, as talking about it is a good first step but it's not enough to move the needle on imposter syndrome in a lasting way.

You must take action despite how you are feeling, despite family dynamics, being the first or only who looks and sounds like you and despite working alone or in a field where competition is high.

When we do decide to take action towards our goals and dreams, our inner imposter often pipes up to ask 'who do you think you are?'

The real question is 'who do you think you are to NOT go for it?'

You are here for a reason, you have skills and a perspective that no one else does, it is your job to share them with others.

You don't have to solve world peace or cure cancer but you can raise your hand for a promotion or to answer a question or throw caution to the wind and follow your dreams. There is always going to be more to learn and discover along the way and this isn't just about you, because nobody wins when bright people play small.

Disclaimer

Rachel Lounds is a confidence coach and imposter syndrome expert. She works with people to overcome imposter syndrome to build confidence in their careers. The information in this article is just a taste of what's inside the *Rethinking Imposter Syndrome*™ workshop and program she delivers.

Rachel Lounds is a Confidence coach and Imposter Syndrome Specialist helping women overcome self doubt and imposter syndrome to reach their career and personal goals.

She is a licenced associate of The Imposter Syndrome Institute, the worlds #1 source of imposter syndrome solutions, to deliver the *Rethinking Impostor Syndrome*™ program, it is her mission to help professional women bridge the confidence gap to become to excel professionally and personally

Rachel loves helping her clients power up their potential to ditch self doubt, find their purpose and maximize their careers and lives through 1:1 coaching, group coaching and interactive workshops.

Mindset Intelligence

Hepburn in Conversation with - **Georgina Pazzi**

I have been researching and working with human behaviour, learning and wellbeing for over three decades. Throughout this time, it was evident that the most profound influence on just about every aspect of our lives is our mindset. Have you ever paused to reflect on your own mindset and how it has impacted where you are right now? With the dawning of a new year, we now have every opportunity to understand our mindset, let go of limiting beliefs, and supercharge our lives to create new and exciting ways to think, believe, and be.

The term 'mindset' refers to our beliefs, our attitudes, and our perceptions about ourselves and our world. Our mindset is a driving force behind our emotions, behaviour, and outcomes. It impacts our relationships, our wellbeing, our health, our wealth, our learning, our success, and our future.

There are different variations of mindsets that you may have heard of. For example: positive or negative mindsets; growth or fixed mindsets; resilient mindsets; entrepreneurial mindsets; and even abundance or scarcity mindsets. What they all have in common is their focus on improving our lives or limiting them.

For many years Dr. Daniel Goleman has shared his research on the importance of Emotional and Social Intelligence including how they support our growth and development. Within our Human Literacy™ education and wellbeing practice and research, we have developed the powerful concept of Mindset Intelligence™ which heavily impacts on both our Emotional and Social Intelligences. To us at Edumazing®, Mindset Intelligence™ is about understanding, regulating, and transforming our mindset, knowing how and when to take charge of our beliefs, attitudes and perceptions, leading ourselves to be in our optimum state in any situation we create or experience.

Voice: Connection and Detachment

One of the four dimensions of Mindset Intelligence™ that has a major influence on us as women, is the power of 'Voice'. From the moment we are born, our mindset is being sculpted by those around us. What we see, feel, and hear, becomes our perceived reality and from this our inner voice is shaped, releasing itself through our words, emotions, and behaviour.

Growing up in a world that has been dominated by male and female stereotypes and expectations others have placed upon us, have created limitations in who we truly are and what we can achieve as women. Through the voices of others, we may have learnt to passively accept instead of actively grow. You may have experienced a voice within you that tells you that you are not enough, or perhaps you don't matter.

Words are more powerful than we can ever imagine. The internal dialogue we have in our heads can bring the best to our day or reduce it to something that compromises our happiness, our wellbeing, and our mental health.

To be mindset intelligent means we need to acknowledge our inner voice. We need to continually connect and recharge ourselves with the beliefs that release our strengths and true nature of who we are as fearless women. We learn to detach from the voices of others that have diminished our self-worth and no longer serve us well.

> ***"A woman who is courageous, vulnerable and resilient has the capacity to develop a Mindset Intelligence™ that can change the world."***
>
> Georgina Pazzi

I know for me this has become a soul-searching yet liberating experience. Although my mother loved me in her own way, she had unachievable expectations of me and made me feel whatever I did was never enough.

As I was growing up, I was continually seeking her approval and more deeply associating this with her love. I came to realise her childhood trauma created a mindset of believing she wasn't enough. This mindset shaped the way she unknowingly parented me.

From this childhood experience I faced many mindset challenges that created an inner voice of not being enough. This manifested into becoming a perfectionist and a workaholic including subconsciously choosing relationships that validated this belief.

As an adult I finally came to the realisation that this inner voice did not belong to me or represent who I am. I understood the power of influence that surrounds us and realised the only way for me to change this belief and others that did not serve me well, was to go within and seek my true voice.

I learnt to detach myself from other's beliefs of me and visually let them go from my thoughts, emotions, and body. Not only did this give me the power to shift my mindset and create my own inner voice that said, "I am enough", it also allowed me to realise I had broken a generational pattern of women within my mother's family who lived with this disabling belief.

Thankfully, I grew from this experience and raised a strong and determined daughter who I love unconditionally knowing she is more than enough. This has now created a mindset intelligent cycle of women within my own family that I'm hopeful will continue for generations to come.

"A mindset intelligent woman, works from the inside out and uses this to positively influence herself and others."

Georgina Pazzi

Mindset Checkin

As part of our continual growth, checking-in to discover the voices in our head that influence our belief system, will allow us to acknowledge the many aspects of ourselves that empower us each day as well as any limitations we create. This offers us renewed opportunities to change what is needed to ensure we continue to thrive and find happiness within.

A mindset check-in, will allow you to uncover the voice that influences you and the beliefs you form about yourself and others that determine the outcome of your experiences. Here's a reflective process you can do to discover your current mindset.

Step 1: Acknowledge

Think of the voices you have heard overtime that are influencing you now. Some may be your own and some may be from others around you. What beliefs have these voices created? Acknowledge the presence of these beliefs and understand that if you need and want to change any of them, firstly you must believe you can.

"Whatever Your Mind Can Conceive and Believe, It Can Achieve." - Napolean Hill

Step 2: Analyse

Go deeper and analyse the impact these beliefs have on your life right now. Do you notice a pattern in your beliefs? Are they empowering you or limiting you? Consider:

- Whose voice(s) shaped this belief
- Why you think you have this belief
- How this belief influences you

Step 3: Alter

If you have a limiting voice and belief that you need and want to change, think of a replacement that will give you a better outcome. For example: You have often heard a voice that tells you your body shape is too big. Your limiting belief may become 'I am obese' or 'I am overweight'. Your actions, including what you focus on, end up validating what you believe whether you are aware of it or not.

If you alter the outcome by catching the voice inside your head and letting it go, then changing this belief to 'I am healthy', your inner voice and focus will begin to relate to this instead. With consistent and deliberate practice, new habits will form overtime that reinforce your new belief. In this example, you will begin to notice healthier eating and exercise habits that confirm your belief and strengthen your Mindset Intelligence™.

"A belief can change if what you need and what you want are aligned."

Georgina Pazzi

Step 4: Act

Your Mindset Intelligence™ will grow if you have small achievable actions in place that you do consistently each day to disempower the limiting voice and create your new belief system. Be kind to yourself as you go through this process as it does take time especially when this belief has been ingrained since your childhood. Remember and apply the 21/90 rule. It takes 21 days to create a new habit and 90 days to make it a permanent habit. Planning simple actions you can take each day that work for you will shift your belief system and unlock the potential of your Mindset Intelligence™.

Daily Mindset Intelligence™ rituals

To support you to act in achievable ways to strengthen your Mindset Intelligence™, consider creating a simple daily Mindset Intelligence™ ritual that will validate your new belief and inner voice. Here are two examples.

Morning sensory activations:

When you wake up in the morning, create opportunities to activate your Mindset Intelligence™ using sensory rehearsals. Use your senses to be exactly who you are at your best related to your mindset intelligent belief. If your belief is 'I am strong', hear this belief in your mind and visualise what this looks like in your body. Move your body stance so that it is strong. Feel yourself breathing in your strength and letting go of self-doubts. See yourself doing something that day that shows you are strong. It could be walking into a scheduled meeting with strength and purpose knowing your voice matters.

Rehearse what you will say. Feel your strength growing and see yourself letting go of other people's judgement and negativity. These daily sensory activations will propel your Mindset Intelligence™ and change your life for the better.

'I am' list:

Instead of a 'To do' list, create an 'I am list' as part of your morning ritual. To begin this on your first morning, write down your new belief and one thing you will do that day to support your belief. You would also say what it is. Be loud and believe it.

For example: I am fearless (belief) because I know and accept who I am and let go of other people's opinions of me (action).

You can continue to add additional actions or change the action you have when you think you have mastered this action in your 'I am' list. It's important not to have too many actions so they become achievable. Stay focused on these and see what happens over time. At the end of the day, look back and celebrate how you achieved your 'I am' list.

So much is possible for you to develop your Mindset Intelligence™ by creating a strong inner voice that represent beliefs that allow you to be your best. Now is an important opportunity to make this happen as the new year commences. What are you waiting for? Sharpen your Mindset Intelligence™ by focusing on the voice you need to empower you and the beliefs that make it happen. You are more than worth it.

Inspirational "Mindset Intelligent' Women: Anne Sullivan and Helen Keller

Improve your our own Mindset Intelligence™. Look for inspirational women that have demonstrated this through their example and how it changed their lives and the lives of others as your motivation.

Two women that have inspired me with their Mindset Intelligence™ are Anne Sullivan and Helen Keller. A powerful way to understand their story is to watch the short video 'Teacher' released by Stephen Covey as part of his book 'The 8th Habit'. (View video at: https://edumazing.info/teachercovey.)

Every time I watch this video and share it with other teachers, we have tears in our eyes realising how important being a teacher is, and how two women living against the odds, found their inner voice and belief to change lives.

Anne Sullivan was almost blind and lived as a ward of the state for four years until she was fourteen. Her determination and belief that she would one day go to school never faltered despite living in an environment where children were not educated. She acted on this belief as soon as she had the opportunity and was allowed to go to Perkins Institution for the Blind for 6 years. She also graduated as valedictorian of her class without any previous formal education.

"True thoughts never lie. I am going to do what they tell me to do. I am going to school. I am not going to be ignorant anymore."

Anne Sullivan

Helen Keller became blind and deaf at 19 months of age. Anne Sullivan became her teacher when she was 7 years old. She taught Helen to communicate by using sign language on her hand and through touch. Although Helen could not hear Anne's voice, her belief in Helen came through her actions and persistence.

"Real independence is attained through your mind and spirit."

Anne Sullivan

This optimistic belief shaped Helen Keller's own Mindset Intelligence™ . Helen Keller became the first blind and deaf person to complete a Bachelor of Art's Degree. She then became an author and speaker supporting the rights of people especially those who were disadvantaged or compromised.

Her unwavering faith in herself and her skills enabled her to empower others thanks to the voice and belief instilled in her by Anne Sullivan.

Amour Propre

1. A belief and confidence in your own ability and value
2. Self-love, self-esteem

Meet Jewellery Designer

Spring Leahy

We had the pleasure of speaking with Spring Leahy jewellery designer, silversmith and owner of boutique jewellery Magpiette. Spring shares her business journey and vision

Please introduce yourself and your label to our readers

I'm Spring Leahy, Founder and Jewellery Designer of Magpiette (pronounced 'mag-pie-eht'). Magpiette is a fine jewellery company, based in Sydney, that is focused on mindfully creating and curating beautiful jewellery with meaning.

When did your love for jewellery and silversmithing start?

I've always been passionate about creating and working with my hands, and have tried so many different creative hobbies and outlets (including painting, ceramics, stained glass, screenprinting, woodwork - to name a few). I started silversmithing about 11-12 years ago - my boyfriend at the time gifted me 2 hours of private tuition with a tutor, which I'd wanted to do for ages. I spent those two hours piercing, filing, hammering, soldering and polishing silver and came out with my first silver ring, and I was hooked - not only to the process but to the beautiful jewellery you get as a result of that effort. I continued to do courses, read books and eventually invested a lot in buying my own tools to continue silversmithing at home.

My love for jewellery really kicked off when I was a teenager. When I was 18, my mum bought me a white gold and diamond ring that I chose, and it was my first 'real' piece of jewellery. I wore it every day for over ten years and it's still one of my most treasured possessions. I also inherited an emerald and diamond ring and earrings when I was 14 from my Grandma - it's not for everyday wear, but I wear the ring every Christmas to keep her close, and in recent years have worn the emerald studs daily.

I realised around that time how meaningful jewellery can be - how it can be a reminder of a special person in your life.

What led you to become a jewellery designer and start your own label? How did your business begin?

It has been a bit of a journey! I started Magpiette 3 years ago, as a bit of an experiment and a side-hustle to my full time job as a Management Consultant. I really just wanted to test it as a potential business, and see if it could work - so I started it out with stocking a few curated collections of pieces by other people, as a way for customers to discover independent jewellery designers.

From there, I then created a new product when the pandemic hit - a DIY jewellery kit where you can design and carve your own ring from jeweller's wax, and then send it back to me to get it cast into silver. I also ran some workshops to teach people how to do wax carving when we were able to do things in person again.

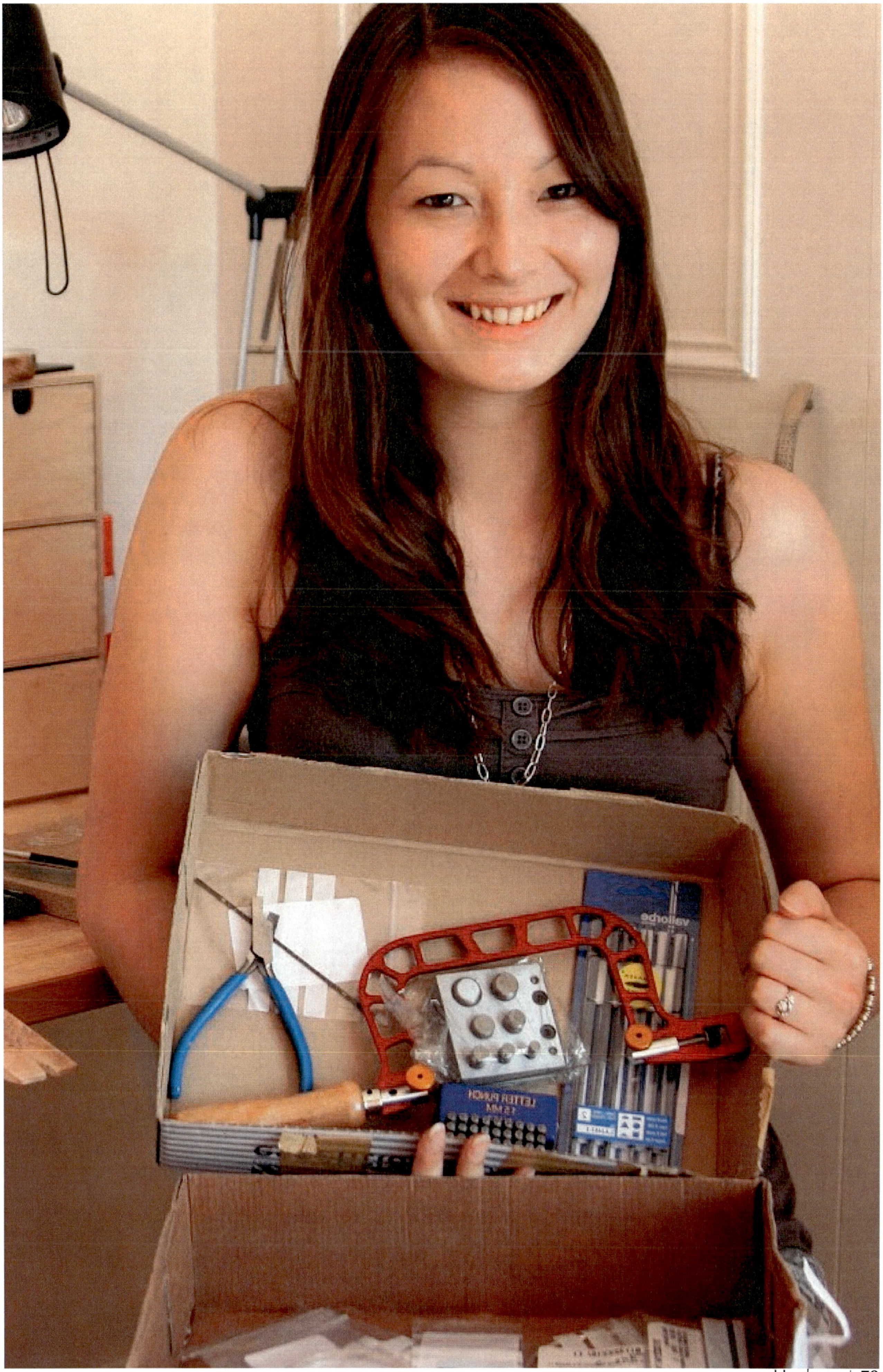

Alongside all this, I realised that I really did want to try launching my own collection. So I took a course in CAD (computer aided design) software and spent some late nights over several weeks learning it over zoom whilst juggling my day job. It's a game changer, because it means I can eventually scale - I can design something once, get it 3D printed and cast in small batches. It needed a lot of time investment and practice though, so it was only recently that I re-learnt it all and now am using it frequently to design jewellery.

When I did finally launch my own collection, it was a mix of pieces made through traditional silversmithing, lost wax casting, and CAD casting. But to have the time to design and make it, I decided to quit my job as a consultant and focus on the work I was most passionate about. It's still early days, but I haven't looked back!

We understand you stock other designers. Could you explain how you choose your designers?

I really wanted to showcase some of the best in the business, so I spent a long time researching independent designers in Australia. I was looking for really unique designs, a high level of craftsmanship and quality, and at a minimum, in sterling silver. I didn't want to stock anything in non-precious metal or that was mass produced or made through being outsourced in Asia. I also knew of a few talented designers in the UK where I'm from, and found one in Portland, USA when I was searching, so I included them too.

Were there any brands or designers that inspired you when you first started Magpiette?

I've always loved Alex Monroe and his whimsical, detailed nature-inspired jewellery, and the brand is also a very inspirational and successful jewellery business to aspire to. In the fine jewellery space, I admire so many designers, but Ruth Tomlinson from the UK is one of my absolute favourites - such a unique style which really complements the amazing gemstones she uses.

What was the main goal you wanted to achieve with your label and have you achieved it yet?

I have so many goals that I want to achieve, and they are all very much work-in-progress. But having just recently taken the plunge to do this full-time, the main goal for me right now is to make this financially sustainable as my main source of income. Once I've achieved that, I'll be able to look towards the future with a bit more certainty.

Describe the Magpiette label in three words. Why these?

Meaning. Craftsmanship. Unique.

We want to create jewellery that holds special meaning for its wearer - whether that's a reminder of a person, place or milestone - rather than creating just another accessory. We care deeply about the creativity and craftsmanship that goes into jewellery design, including all of our own designs and those of the designers we stock. And finally, we want to design and sell the most unique and beautiful jewellery - we aren't interested in being the same as everyone else.

What are the highlights of your business so far?

The highlights for me have been getting to design and make bespoke engagement rings for customers - there's something incredibly rewarding and creative about that process. It means I also get to source and play with incredible gemstones, such as a 3ct pink Padparadscha sapphire, which is the rarest type of sapphire. And then knowing that the piece will be worn everyday for a lifetime is very cool.

What advice would you give to your younger self or upcoming jewellers just starting their career?

Take all the opportunities you can to learn and put yourself out there - and just get started as soon as you can.

Starting a brand is only one side of the business. What are some of the unexpected business challenges you have faced?

I've been surprised at how tough it can be mentally to start a business; I wasn't expecting the anxiety and loneliness that can come with it some days. But one unexpected challenge definitely tops the list - I was overdue on doing my taxes for a couple of years and kept putting it off because I knew how massive a task it was to pull all my new business transactions together.

I finally forced myself to do it, spending weeks on it - and saved it all in a .csv file (working in a downloaded statement file from my bank). I didn't realise that file format erases all tabs except your last one, and there's no version recovery! It was very painful to have to do all that work again...ouch!

Where do you see yourself and the Magpiette brand in 10 years?

Hopefully I'll still be doing this! I think Magpiette could go in one of two directions as it grows - either focusing more on bespoke engagement rings, or more on the collections side. Either way, in ten years I'd love to have built it up to a small team with my own retail space or two... that would be a dream.

Pink Padparadscha sapphire and diamond engagement ring in 18ct rose gold

Paperclip Chain Necklace by Magpiette

Meet Fashion Designer
Sarah Lloyd

Meet Sarah Lloyd. Sarah is a successful Sydney based fashion designer who has created her own label and fashion business. Hepburn has to pleasure of interviewing Sarah to find out more about her and the Sarah Lloyd fashion label.

Please introduce yourself to our readers:

Sarah Lloyd is a Sydney based fashion designer producing timeless designer pieces for the style conscious woman of today. Designed and made in Australia, the label's signature aesthetic embodies sophistication with a focus on quality and classic design.

Before focusing on design, I worked with leading fashion designers, including the late Carla Zampatti and Leona Edmiston. I gained industry experience and an understanding of the lifestyle needs of the modern Australian woman. Drawing on experience, I design to create confidence through a refined selection of timeless foundation styles.

I sell ready to wear collections online, as well as made to order designs. Seasonally, I host intimate events from my studio inviting women to preview new pieces and find out more about the label. The studio doubles as a show- room for women to book private appointments, preview collections, and try on designs and discuss bespoke designs.

When did your love of fashion start?

At an early age I was making dresses for Barbie, hand sewing dresses for myself and altering existing pieces in my wardrobe.

What led you to start your own fashion label and business?

I've always designed and loved design. I think you are born a designer. Starting my own label was an extension and expression of whom I am. Personally I felt ready after having had my children and having gained experience working in the industry for a number of years.

What are some of the highlights of your career so far?

Being able to do what I love. Designing pieces that make women feel beautiful.

Please share how you implement ethical and sustainable practices into your fashion business?

The Sarah Lloyd label has a strong focus on sustainable fashion. I have a passion for sustainable fashion, enthusing quality over quantity, and designing for longevity in the lives of women's wardrobes. I deliver boutique collections with a focus on timeless design and made to order pieces. The overall aim is ensuring zero waste, with a considered approach to style.

Honesty and transparency promote trust. I want the women who buy Sarah Lloyd to know what I stand for and trust the brand.

What advice would you give to your younger self or those aspiring designers?

Trust your instinct. Be brave. Be bold. Surround yourself with an army of support. The fashion industry isn't for the faint hearted.

Where do you see yourself and your label in 10 years?

I'd like to see the label become recognised internationally with signature showrooms in London, Sydney, and Melbourne.

Finally, describe Sarah Lloyd in three words. Why these?

Timeless sophistication. Australian. First words embody my design aesthetic. The last word, I'm proudly Australian and love that my product is made locally.

Sarah Lloyd

Sarah designs elegant and sophisticated pieces for the Australian woman.

She designs pieces from sizes 6-16 as well as custom-made orders for sizes 6-16 plus. This is ideal for those who want to be fitted and customise their chosen garment. We had the pleasure to interview Sarah on her career, business, and future ambitions for her label Sarah Lloyd.

"We carry the story of the people who made our clothes."

– Ali Hewson

Notes

Q&A with *Chamani*

Isabella Stephan

Introducing successful fashion designer Chamani Weerasekara who designs timeless garments with a sustainable and conscious approach. We had the pleasure of interviewing the Brisbane-based designer about her label CHAMANI.

Please introduce yourself to our readers?

My name is Chamani, the founder and designer behind my namesake, purpose-driven label CHAMANI. CHAMANI is a conscious luxury, wearable activism brand that fights for freedom, equality and opportunity for marginalised women, girls and communities through timeless, thoughtful wearable art. CHAMANI is more than just a brand but a movement. To manufacture our collections, we partner with talented artisans to create our beautiful custom fabrics – each hand-dyed and hand-woven using sacred and ancient techniques passed down through generations.

When did your love for fashion start?

From a young age, I would spend days and hours sketching my dream designs, getting lost in magazines and watching runway shows on TV, completely inspired by the incredible fashion on display.

Growing up, my beautiful grandmother and aunt would foster my creativity and help bring my ideas and designs to life.

What led you to become a fashion designer and start your own label?

Whilst living in South East Asia, I saw the effects of fast, cheap, unsustainable fashion first-hand. I saw the pollution it caused to our waterways and the amount of landfills it created. I met people who had been wronged by an industry. Rather than causing such detrimental effects on people and our planet, it should be creating impactful, positive change with its enormous and incredible power. I knew I wanted to be a part of the change, and I knew I had to do something.

How did your fashion business begin?

Combining the magic of my recent working holiday in South East Asia and love for helping people and timeless fashion, I began my journey to founding my impact-led business. Within a couple of months of moving back to Australia, I was booking a flight to India to meet with artisans, fabric suppliers and potential manufacturers. There were so many ups and downs, twists and turns, especially during the pandemic, so it took almost two years to finally get to launch day! I truly learned everything on the job, made lots of mistakes, spent hours researching and educating myself and began connecting with people in the industry.

Describe the CHAMANI label in three words.

Conscious luxury, and wearable-activism.

Could you tell us how important it is to be a sustainable brand?

Hugely important. People and the planet are at the core of every decision made within the business. Currently, fashion is incredibly detrimental to our planet.

Through CHAMANI, I want to show that we can make beautiful fashion while being kind to our planet and fellow humans.
Starting a fashion label is only one side of the business. What are some of the unexpected business challenges you have faced?

Trying to do everything "right" in the fashion industry has proven to be incredibly difficult and continues to be challenging, as the systems are not in place for this type of fashion. It can be incredibly time-consuming (and costly) to source and use all sustainably and ethically sourced materials.

What are some of the highlights of your career so far?

1. The day I launched our first collection — a momentous day
2. Having two pop-up stores with the support of Brisbane Fashion Month, and being showcased at their incredible runway show later in the year
3. And the brand [CHAMANI] being featured in some amazing publications, such as British Vogue.

Were there any brands or designers you looked up to when you first started CHAMANI?

I think my main inspiration has been small artisan groups that I've met on my travels. I adore the sacred techniques and skills that have been passed down through generations.

What advice would you give to your younger self or any upcoming fashion designers?

Believe in your vision and stay true to your WHY. Trust in the journey and know that everyone's path is different. Just know that YOU are the secret ingredient to your label and no other label has YOU.

Where do you see yourself and your label in 10 years?

I'd love CHAMANI to be an internationally recognised label not just for fashion but as a symbol of wearable activism and women empowerment. It would be an absolute dream to be in some beloved bespoke boutique stores all over the world that stock independent designers.

To find out more about Chamani or to shop her luxurious and beautifully designed pieces, head to chamani.com.au

DO NOT CHANGE BOBBIN CASE

Q&A with *Astille*

Isabella Stephan

Introducing successful fashion designer Sallyanne Astill who designs timeless garments. We had the pleasure of interviewing the Brisbane-based designer about her label Astille.

Please introduce yourself to our readers?

I am Sallyanne Astill and I am a Brisbane based fashion designer. I started my label Astille in 2018 after finishing my (fourth) degree at Torrens University in Brisbane. I spent many years in the tech industry as a software engineer and felt a little like a sore thumb as someone fashionable in a digital world where I was surrounded by corporate suits or tracksuits and hoodies. I dreamt of following my passion for travel and culture through the lens of a fashion designer. Astille is a ready to wear label inspired by the old Hollywood silhouettes reimagined in a modern world, made from beautiful fabrics and prints. Each collection is created from a French inspired theme that is woven into every seam and in house designed print.

When did your love for fashion start?

As a child I was always drawing fashion illustrations. My love affair with clothes and expressing myself dressing up began early. To be honest it is all I ever wanted was to be a fashion designer. I didn't however follow my passion until much later in life. Coming from an academic family I was encouraged to get a degree that would guarantee a job. I ended up studying computer science. A career in software engineering was creative in its own way, but ultimately it wasn't a passion.
I got to a point where I thought you only live once so I thought let's give it a shot! I'm not known to do things by halves so I researched the best place to study and made inroads with some of Australia's best contacts in the fashion industry

What led you to become a fashion designer and start your own label?

After completing my degree in Branded Fashion, I felt comfortable with interacting with the industry and set about building my network. I assessed my skillset and realised I needed a small team to support this huge vision of mine. That's when I started working with The New Garde, a small but mighty team that understands my visions and supports the journey.

Were there any brands or designers that you looked to when you first started Astille?

Carla Zampatti and her daughter Bianca Spender are truly an admirable family of talent. I also admire, Ulla Johnson for her wanderlust bohemian creations, and Alexander McQueen for the sheer brilliance and superbly crafted off beat designs. Australia has some wonderful designers also. Brands like McGraw and KitX are super cool and focus on efforts toward sustainability.

We understand that the French culture has inspired Astille. Could you tell us how?

French women are my muse - for their nonchalant confidence and their undeniable ability to comprise an outfit sourced from almost anywhere. They are not driven by trends or brands necessarily, yet they can transcend style itself - authentic and comfortable dressing, impossibly chic! If I could I buy a plane ticket to France over and over and immerse myself in the history, the art, food and theatre. My time there was always spent well with admiring the art, the architecture and how people interact, how community and passion is a way of life. This ethos is woven into every garment and transcends my personal experience.

What was the main goal you wanted to achieve with your label and have you achieved it yet?

I believe it is a creative journey and I am excited to see where Astille can go! I have a lot more to achieve and really, I'm only just getting started post covid. I am growing the business and loving the customer interaction I have. So far, it's all been priceless and something I treasure every day, to be able to wake up and design for women who genuinely want to express their style in a non-chalant way, just like those gorgeous French women I feel connected with.

Describe the Astille label in three words. Why these?

Unique, Modern, Authentic.

Each Astille piece is unique, it has a modern feel, it feels great to wear and it feels like you!

What are the highlights of your career so far?

The runway shows, and collection launches have been pivotal moments for me so far. Meeting new clients and getting their positive feedback is a source of joy for me. I love to make things that people want to wear, that is exciting. Women of all ages are beautiful, they can all wear something a little unique or different, focussing on parts of the body that are often neglected, shoulders, necks, waists, and ankles for example. I am looking forward to many more highlights as Astille grows with me. But right now, it's all about the little community I have come to love.

What advice would you give to your younger self or any upcoming fashion designers?

It is never too late to do what you love! Do what you want to do if you have a passion for something. Live to work, not work to live - is an adage that really rings true for me. Have faith in yourself and your abilities. It is a tough industry, but that passion will steer you a long way to being successful.

What advice would you give to your younger self or any upcoming fashion designers?

Fashion is not an easy industry to be in, you have to love what you do. There is so much invested up front in development and production, and there is definitely an element of risk. The main challenge that was totally unexpected was COVID, how do you mitigate against the effects of a global pandemic, especially in terms of international supply chain operations, staffing shortages and people in isolation? All of this was outside my control, as well as navigating the challenges that already face fashion start-ups.

Where do you see yourself and your label in 10 years?

I see Astille growing steadily and organically growing over the next 10 years, onboarding a number of carefully selected wholesale clients, with a thriving online presence, and some strategic overseas stockists. I would also consider an Astille branded bricks and mortar retail store somewhere local in Brisbane at some stage. I see myself still at the helm, working with a great team of people supporting Astille in its journey.

In Conversation

Hepburn Series

Upcoming In Conversations

Hepburn Series

We have a great lineup of Amazing and Aspiring women coming this year, including:

Jean Adams of Business & Empowerment Mentor,

Stephanie Bofinger of Fempro Armour

Elena Pa of Gyre Australia, and

Ruby Schmidt of Toy Shop Entertainment

We invite you to subscribe to our YouTube channel and Podcasts to listen to future episodes.

Subscribe to Hepburn YouTube and podcasts

MAKING YOUR NEXT MOVE?

READY TO LEAD? READY TO LEAD?

WWW.GALE.EDU.AU
STUDY@GALE.EDU.AU
0421 571 381

GALE

Global Academy of Leadership and Entrepreneurship

Enquire about our
Leadership and Business Courses

RTO41404

Passion
1. Any powerful or compelling emotion or feeling, as love or hate
2. A strong or extravagant fondness, enthusiasm, or desire for anything

Meet Cathryn Mora
Author and Publisher

Words: Cathryn Mora

"You should write a book about your life," people would often say to me. I knew my path hadn't exactly been conventional, but given that I was still an absolute nobody in the eyes of the world, who would want to read my story?

I don't think I ever fit the model of an employee, but that's what we're prepared for at school, so I did my best to follow that path. I studied Film and Television Production as a major at university, with a minor in Marketing, and fortunately it fell under the banner of business, so I technically ended up with a business degree.

As soon as I left university, I wanted to travel. I didn't even try to get into the film industry, even though Warner Bros. had just opened a studio an hour away on the Gold Coast, Australia. My justification was that since I was going overseas, that there was no point me trying to get into the industry; that I should just get a temp office job and save money for my trip, and then I'd go head first into finding film work upon my return. A fellow student had just landed a position as an intern at Warner Bros., but I needed money for my trip to London, so an unpaid position was of no interest to me.

Within weeks of arriving in London, I landed a job on a cruise ship in the Caribbean. I didn't last terribly long, but ended up in London for years after that. Once I got home, five years had passed since I graduated, and my film industry contacts had long since dried up.

So I just gave up on that dream I guess. I had spent my London years working in roles loosely related to marketing, and back in Brisbane, I was able to forge a decent career in marketing, communications, and media. For years I tried to find happiness in contract work, and while my income was fine, I never reached any level of true fulfilment.

Seven years after I arrived home, when my relationship failed, I left Australia again, this time for longer. I went back to work on cruise ships for a while, then moved to Paris, where I gained six kilograms in a couple of months due to my habit of drinking wine and eating daily tarte au citron. Paris was a bit full-on for me. I love it as a city, but my social circle liked to party with nose candy, and that was never my scene.

I made my way back to London and spent a couple of years training in performance and trying to forge a career in the West End as a singer in musicals. As part of that journey, I joined a full-time dance program in New York City, and lived there while attempting to channel my inner Carrie in a Sex and the City lifestyle.

Turns out I'm a decent singer but not professional musical theatre standard, and when the GFC hit in 2008, the annual rush of auditions dried up and I took a job as the resident entertainer in a holiday park in Cornwall. I met a young South American man and got swept up in a whirlwind romance. When the controlling resort owner cottoned onto our relationship, she started making our lives difficult, so he proposed after six weeks and we ran away in the middle of the night. Him to a new job in Scotland, and me to open a tanning and lash salon in London.

It was my first taste of business ownership and it didn't last long. I got bored with the day to day running of the operation, and we ended up moving to Ecuador to get married. It turns out that being a gringa in South America can be trying and exhausting, and we finally moved to my home of Brisbane and had a baby.

My father had been a true entrepreneur. He grew up in poverty and left school at the age of twelve to work and contribute to the family. He was of the era where hard work paid off, and combined with his brilliant brain, he built a multi-million-dollar computer networking business. I was a teenager at that time, so completely absorbed in my own world, but I did observe that the success didn't bring him much happiness either. A bigger business meant more stress, and when he suddenly went bankrupt during my university years it had a big impact on me. Losing his money knocked the thin veil of self-confidence he'd managed to build, and he didn't want to live anymore. He didn't deliberately cause his own demise, but he didn't take care of himself and died from liver disease in his 60s.

Through therapy I've had in recent years, I realised that my dad's journey had significantly curtailed any entrepreneurial dreams I may have allowed myself to have. It wasn't conscious at the time, but I now know that my subconscious thought process was, If he wanted to kill himself over losing his money, then I never want money to be so important.

And I was very successful at not making money!

In all those years of travelling and working in government, not for profit, and corporate, I still lived week to week for the most part, and still turned up to work every day feeling sick in the pit of my stomach. I would attend meetings where people were passionately discussing the latest work project, and I'd often be thinking, Why do any of you even care?

I still had dreams of writing a book, but the timing was never right, and I didn't quite know what I'd write anyway.

When my son was born, I thought, Well, since I'm about to have all this spare time (can you tell I was optimistically delusional?!) I may as well write that book.

Instead of writing about my life, I had decided to write a novel, influenced by my time on cruise ships – called Sex, Lies, and Cruising. Every time I felt motivated or inspired, I'd sit down and write... but it turns out that when you have a baby and a full-time job, life just isn't that inspiring much of the time. I wrote only eight chapters in 20 months.

People would say, "What happened to your book?" "Weren't you writing a book?" "Aren't you finished it yet?"

I wished I'd never even mentioned the stupid book!

My husband said, "Are you going to finish it? You don't want to wake up at 70 and say, 'Damn, I wish I'd written that book...'" and he was so right. I don't feel like I should ever regret the things I've done, but I certainly don't want to be left with regret for the things I didn't do!

I signed up to work with a mentor, wrote for at least 15 minutes every day, whether I felt like it or not, and finished the last 13 chapters in ten weeks. It was the absolute greatest and proudest moment of my entire life. Finishing the first draft of a book while looking after a baby and working full-time, I felt like Superwoman!

After many, many rounds of self-editing and professional editing over a six month period, I tried to get a publishing deal and was rejected across the board. I was devastated. I'd put years into this book and nobody wanted it. One professional appraisal I paid for said, "Don't ever show anybody this book." I opened THAT email on the first day of a family holiday!

WRITE
CATHRYN MORA
THE RIGHT STAFF
D.A. SPENCE
SOUL MODES
SEX LIES & CRUISING
DEZIEL
THE CONTENTFUL FRAMEWORK
ADOPT & EMBRACE MICROSOFT TEAMS
Flowers and Honey
Julie Tenner
Letter to my 10-year-old self
AN ANTHOLOGY

I put the book to the side for six months. I was exhausted and my spirit was feeling broken from the barrage of rejection.

But I'm not a quitter.

I went back to the book, hired another editor, edited it again, and self-published it to rave reviews. I hired a publicist and was in 23 outlets in 20 days, including flying to Sydney for television news, featuring in many online news outlets, appearing on multiple radio shows and print media like Cosmopolitan magazine.

I leveraged that media coverage to strike a deal with Big W – Australia's largest book retailer – and from there negotiated a distribution deal with a distributor. Very rare for a self-published author. My book appeared in book shops around the country, including airport bookshops, and travelling friends would send me photos from different airports around Australia of my book proudly displayed on the shelves.

The book was successful in terms of sales and media coverage, but it didn't quite make enough money for me to live on a tropical island for the rest of my life... so I was still stuck in a job I didn't love, and fighting the urge to quit every day.

Eventually, I quit anyway. I hated the way I felt on the 40-minute drive to work each day, and would sit in the carpark for ten minutes every morning, just to gather the energy to go inside. There wasn't anything terribly wrong with the job; it was just that I wasn't feeling any inspiration or fulfillment. I didn't feel aligned or happy, ever.

One day my husband came home with a flyer about a coaching diploma being run at the Southbank TAFE in Brisbane. I had never even heard of coaching, but it looked fascinating, and I signed up. On my first day, I was in tears. I had never seen anything so powerful. And by the second day, the teacher said to me, "You are a natural. You could start charging today."

After graduating, I excitedly created a brand and started my coaching business. I started with relationship coaching, which flopped, along with the relationship SMS program I had invested about $40,000 into. I thought, I've come this far. I can't give up now... and changed my focus to career coaching. Another flop.

Frustrated, I hired a business coach. She said, "What are you most proud of? What have you done that lights you up when you think about it?"

I didn't have to think hard about that... writing my book and finishing the first draft. Even though I'd had all that media and excitement around my launch, just writing the book was still my greatest and proudest achievement. "I want to help other people achieve that feeling," I said.

My book coaching business was born. Since January 2018 I've been helping people write non-fiction books, like self-help and memoir, and many of them have forged careers as professional speakers, and met new clients or charged more for their coaching, because writing and publishing a quality book positions you as an authority and expert in your industry.

Every time my client finishes their first draft and says, "I finally finished! I never thought I'd see the day!" I am reminded why I do this. It's the greatest honour of my life to help people share their stories. I've been privileged to hear the most private and difficult moments of people's lives, and help turn them into a story which will engage and captivate readers. And that's really down to the commitment, bravery, and trust of my authors.

COVID presented some big challenges for me, as my entire speaker base was wiped. I had to think fast, and created an online course, and started compiling high quality anthologies, as a way of becoming more accessible to people who wanted to write, but perhaps didn't have the time, energy, or budget to invest into my 1:1 programs. I didn't exactly sail through, and my

mum paid my mortgage one month, but I did make it through.

This year I've had some good news. My novel from all those years ago has been optioned by a production company, and one of the world's biggest film companies, which has created a TV network, is looking at our show at the time of writing this. This means there is a chance my book will be made into a TV show, and I will be the creator, as well as a writer on the production team.

From there, I'd love to write some more books and have them made into film. Once one show is made, it opens up a whole new world of opportunity - and that is mind blowing to me.

The optimistic girl who applied to study film and television production way back in 1991 might finally be getting her dream.

And that is worth every moment of the entire journey.

The Resilient Carer

Tasha Doucas

Words: Julia Jerg

"The shift from a state of DOing into a state of BEing frees one from lack; lack of time, energy, or self worth. BEing envelops oneself in abundance, as a beacon for light, love, and healing."

Caring doesn't stop for the caregiver especially over the holidays. Caregiving is round the clock, 24fl - 365 days of the year of care and compassion, worry and concern, fatigue and exhaustion, organizing and planning, and love and tenderness.

It's not just the patient that is going through the journey of their illness, disease, or injury. It affects every part of the family ecosystem.

Tasha's mission is to bring more ease, harmony, energy, and deeper connection for the Carer in their Family Caregiving journey.

Tasha is a Resilient Caregiver. She is a mother and life partner and has been a family caregiver for well over a decade.

Who is Tasha Doucas

In Tasha's lifetime she has cared for both her parents, her husband and her son. She is currently caring for her husband through his cancer journey and their teenage boy diagnosed with ADHD. She now achieves everything she sets out to achieve with more grace, resilience, and harmony than she ever thought possible. And she did it all while going through her own personal life struggles early on suffering burnout, lack of self care, and growing resentment.

She used to think:

I can do it myself! and that Asking for help is a sign of weakness!

Having control over situations leads to more peace, greater efficiency, and more time. Caregivers are meant to be generous with the time and acts of service.

Tasha has written and published her eBook The Feminine Carer Way as her contribution to all Women seeking support to deepen their carer relationship.

She works with her clients to allow them to step into more flow, abundance, better health and vibration as well as a deeper connection with the one you are supporting and caring for.

Tasha uses the Feminine approach to caregiving which is a far more emotional approach, involving feeling and connection, and vulnerability in addressing differences or conflict resolution [for stress release], to allow for more flow, throughout the journey.

Where it started:

In 2006, both her parents were diagnosed, a month apart, with two different kinds of cancer types. This, without her being aware, started Tasha on her journey of caregiver and now as Caregiver Life Coach.

Year later Tasha cared through her mom's journey with Dementia for nine years. During the same time in Tasha's life, she was raising a young family, as the predominant breadwinner. She was clearly juggling a lot in her life. When her mother finally moved into a care facility, Tasha stepped up her heightened level of intuition, observation, and her sensitivity to energy around her.

With her mother's care, once Tasha accepted the WHAT IS in the moment, she was able to sit with, feel the surrounding energy, and BE with her mother. When she stepped foot into that Care facility, it was all about the emotion of loving, fun, joyous energy. She would wrap her arms around her mother and say the biggest I LOVE YOU, MOM!

Yes, it wasn't easy to see her mother's condition worsen over time, not being able to understand her surroundings, lose her speech, and regress to childlike behaviors. But she wanted to give her mother the most positive energy she possibly could and enjoy those special moments.

Tasha made a decision and chose to LET GO!

Most recently Tasha was a full time caregiver for her life partner on his journey with Non-Hodgkin's Lymphoma. With her husband's care, when his cancer returned more aggressively, Tasha let go of control and asked her partner what path he saw for his treatment, his vision for this journey to play out, and how he thought it best for her to best support him and provide care. This is an example of Creating Space.

Tasha has now quit her corporate job to follow her soul's calling to coach Family Caregivers and help them shift into a more feminine approach.

The Need for a Different Approach - The Feminine Carer Way

Many Caregivers tend to embody the word careGIVER. And the GIVER side of the role has us living in the DOing energy. This DO energy is controlled by lists, appointments, research, health checks and follow ups, cooking, taxes, financial and estate planning and the list going on... and on... and on. The "job" of the caregiver never feels done.

Tasha believes every caregiver needs a balance of both the feminine and masculine energy, however we tend to start off our caregiver journey in the masculine energy ruled by lists, schedules, research, etc. And this is where we can be led down the path of overwhelm, fatigue, and resentment if we stay solely in this energy too long.

It is easy to get overwhelmed with tons of information and then one tends to ask themselves "how will I manage everything?"

What if we could evolve to a more preventative approach to fight off caregiver burnout and change the mindset to a more soulful, intimate and energy-rising caregiver role?

The Carer Languages

We all come from different worlds and backgrounds, different parents, generational stories we carry, and our true essence of our soul. The Languages we use with each other are critical to connection. Tasha has introduced three new Carer Languages further evolving the Carer relationship:

Vulnerability - is sharing something that is so deep and private with the other person that it closes the GAP and builds a sense of common appreciation and kindness.

Generosity - they like to create memorable experiences, it could be overly generous gifts or hand-picked experiences that bring delight to the other person, as they feel deeply cherished.

Creating Space - they like creating space for peace and harmony, sometimes it is finding free time so that higher priorities can be addressed. It is the basis of self-care and creating moments for it.

Caregiving is 24/7 but the Family Caregiver doesn't have to feel overwhelmed, burned out, and feel like it won't ever end. Tasha helps women Family Carers to bring more ease into their journey, and learning how to "fill their bucket".

She also focuses on navigating the family communication side of things, as triggers from the past and our childhood do often come up when tensions are felt during challenging times.

Are you ready to heal from all these negative emotions and step into resiliency, uplifting energy and more intimacy with oneself and with those around you?

Connect with Tasha to learn more about The Resilient Carer Program. Get your copy of her eBook and take the Resilient Carer Questionnaire to explore your caregiver journey. Go to www.theresilientcarer.com

Aspiring Australian Women
Tina Haywood

Words: Julia Jerg

Turning the roles from being a victim to becoming responsible for your personal happiness and re-writing your own story despite the challenges that life puts in your way is something not many people choose to do. It's not an easy option to choose, probably that's why. It takes courage, it takes realization, it may be painful and in the first place, it requires awareness - which can only be gained by focusing on what is inside yourself.

Tina Haywood is one of those fighters who overcame trauma and turned her suffering into power, resilience and a mission:

> ***"My goal is to help women escape domestic violence and sexual assault and to become strong, self-sufficient warriors who can return home and lead their communities into the future."***

The mother who wears many hats, who is a mum, a business owner, a mentor, keynote speaker and a strong resilient leader is with her program called BluebutterflySkye - a transformational complete empowerment program that aims to promote the following rebirth, hope, and bravery for target audience impacted by Suicide, specifically aimed at Indigenous/ ATSI community, Youth and DV victims.

The symbolism of a butterfly is the foundation of BlueButterflySky which was chosen as "***Butterflies show us how we can go within ourselves to dissolve old forms and morph, rebuilding and evolving ourselves,***" she explains, noting that they show us the importance of surrender and trust "***as part of the essential process of growth and renewal.***"

'I want to inspire ladies and families in the community and around Australia to help them shine and gain back their powers that once were taken and help them build their resilience , self esteem and happiness back up. It's a journey Of healing , empowering, building beautiful souls up and I am passionate about doing something I love.'- Tina Haywood

The techniques and healing sessions during the program focus on the support for women to break out of the negative thought patterns that have been passed down through the generations. They get a deeper awareness of intergenerational trauma and grow in wisdom. These gatherings give them a chance to look back on the successes and failures of previous efforts, as well as to chart a course for the future. By pooling the collective expertise in a safe environment, her clients can all talk openly about what has worked and what hasn't.

Tina explains: I am really passionate about my work and enjoy doing what I love. One crucial element of it is to listen. Because a single discussion may change a person's life, we must listen and allow others to be heard, share our knowledge, and transform evidence into action.

The business BlueButterflyskye was born when she wrote her book and began to share her personal story to provide empowerment to the community and facilitate change. As of today, Tina Haywood has impacted hundreds of women's lives across Australia and is working on scaling her business by adding more supportive materials to her portfolio such as books, courses and workshops and healing camps. She is actively sharing her message in keynote speaking for community events and virtually on Instagram and Facebook to help increase awareness of the topics that she touches on.

And if that wasn't already enough, the power woman wears many hats: Aside from being a mother, and business owner, she is also a mentor for the indigenous soldiers in Department of Defence's Australian Army who has been serving for 9 and half years and Author as well as Trauma Healer and advocate for survivors of domestic violence and sexual assault and keynote speaker. Her past experiences and current work has given her an unique perspective on the challenges women, families and youth face today.

I hear your cries and feel your tears... you have been praying for a simple clear pathway to get your power back and not be afraid to make decisions that truly matter I will help you grow your inner strength again.

It's not your fault, but it is your responsibility to change it.

The woman of Australian aboriginal identity, explains her vision and mission in powerful way:

'Its a community obligation to change suicide for the next generation, that addresses both prevention and early intervention to manage feeling and develop emotional resilience for vulnerable young people and adults.' Tina is publishing her next work this November, the BlueButterfly Journal. This key resource includes engaging children in stress reduction tools and bridging the gap for Aboriginal /ATSI youth in strengthening the connection to country and tradition. It builds on self-love practices, journaling and healing practices and self-love affirmations aimed at helping youth to learn to build in love and Break the Cycle.

Tina Haywood is proud Yupungathi/ Gangalidda woman and a survivor of trauma and a spokesperson for the prevention of youth suicide and social and emotional well-being. The business BlueButterflyskye was born when she wrote her book and began to share her personal story to provide empowerment to the community and facilitate change.

GALE

READY FOR YOU READY FOR YOU
WWW.GALE.EDU.AU
STUDY@GALE.EDU.AU

GLobal Academy of
Leadership and Entrepreneurship

RTO 41404

Enquire about our
Professional Writing Courses

WWW.GALE.EDU.AU
STUDY@GALE.EDU.AU

MEET THE FUTURE YOU

STRONG
FREE
EDUCATED
CREATIVE

Leisure

1. Freedom from the demands of work or duty
2. Unhurried ease

"Women have to
harness their power—
it's absolutely true.
It's just learning not
to take the first no.
And if you can't go
straight ahead, you go
around the corner."

—**Cher**

It's About Their Safety

Hepburn in Conversation with - Stephanie Bofinger

This month, we were delighted be speak with Stephanie Bofinger, founder and inventor of Fempro Armour, body armour for female motor cyclists. Stephanie a former Olympian swimmer immigrated to Australia at the age of 20 with very little English but a lot of determination to succeed.

What led you to developing Fempro Amour?

So in 2019, I rode my dirt bike through the Simpson Desert with a bunch of girls to raise money for Dolly's Dream in the charity event. And whilst going over 1200 sand dunes, trying to stay alive, I realized that my personal problem with protective gear was being shared amongst the other girls. One of the riders didn't wear any protective gear because she said it is so uncomfortable that she rather wear nothing than being distracted by the discomfort. Whilst riding across the desert,

I had an idea come to my thoughts. So after four days, I came to the conclusion that no one is going to change how females in impact sports are protected. So I'm going have to do it myself. And I told my partner at the time, 'I'm going to design female body armour...I have no freaking idea, but I will figure it out'. And, so 12 months and four days later we launched our first product and our company at the time was called Miss XG because it was more about dirt biking in motorcycle. Yes. But then we fairly, soon understood that the problem that we motorcyclists had was pretty much in every impact sports. So we rebranded Miss MXG into, and FemPro Amour.

It was a big challenge to develop Fempro But it's also a big challenge to cross the Simpson Desert on a motorcycle. Tell us a little about that adventure.

When I originally heard about the women crossing the Simpson Desert, let's say, I've always tried to do things that people usually don't do. There is, an element of excitement that not many, do it. It's different. And whilst I hate being in my outside zone, it's not, in my comfortable zone, but I do like it. I like pushing myself. So when I heard about this ride, I'm going, wouldn't it be great to do this. And, when

MissMxG
Miss

I, reached out, unfortunately the ride was full. I'm a true believer that things are meant to happen when they're happening. And, a few months later I received a call, a girl has pulled out. There's one opening. That was in June.

I had only rode sand once before. That time I had hit a tree and couldn't ride for a number of months. So really I had no experience about how to ride sand but it excited me to do. It scared me but that was also the excitement behind it. We did prepare with some training. As you know, everything comes down to preparation.

It felt like we had overtrained because it became quite easy at the start. But it's the whole atmosphere and not knowing what is ahead of you when you go over a sand dune. It is scary because the Simpson Desert changes with every day. You know, it doesn't look the same the next day. There's obviously four wheel drive cars coming across you and meeting people. And, then the solitude of the Simpson Desert is amazing. The whole experience was incredible. It's certainly something.

How long does the ride across the Simpson Desert take?

We took quite a long time. It was nearly four days, but that's only because when you arrive with your dirt bike you have only a small tank. So we could not go too far away from the support vehicles that had the fuel. But the problem is we ride at about 60, 70 kilometres an hour over because you have to have a certain speed, so you're not digging yourself into the sand. But the cars would only go around 20kms. So you were waiting. It felt like it took forever for the cars to get where we were, so we could fuel up and keep going.

You can ride the Simpson Desert if you're an experienced rider and you have extra fuel and you have a larger tank within a day. But it's a full on day and it's not for someone that is a beginner rider, or even an intermediate. You have to be an advanced rider to cross the Simpson Desert in one hit.

You've highlighted that you like to do things that are a little out of the ordinary and things that people don't usually attempt. Is there something that you're really passionate about?

Well, riding one of my passions. One of my passions to push myself beyond the limit that normally people would give up. And I guess that comes from my sporting background as a professional swimmer. So I had to obviously push myself each day in training to get the maximum out of my body. So I've never learned to take things the normal way. So for me it's always either the 'completely off' or the 'complete extreme'. And, I'm very passionate about motorcycling.

It's my escape. I can think. I have my solitude. It's where I charge up my batteries. When I'm not feeling a hundred percent, I go on my motorcycle and two hours later I feel like, nothing happened before.

I'm most definitely passion about motorcycling. Working in the space of what I do with Fempro Armour and being involved in motorcycling, I don't feel like I really work. I'm very fortunate to have found something that I'm passionate and I can do this 24 hours, seven days a week. Which has a bad side to it as well, because I never stop.

You don't stop. You don't have a down downside to your life, but for the present, that Is okay.

What happens if, um, something fails though? Have you thought about what alternatives you might pursue?

I don't have a plan B. I am a great believer that you either have one plan or no plan. A plan B is an escape. If something doesn't work for me, I'm going to try everything to make it work. There is no escape route. There is no option for me. It's this is going to work and it's up to me to

Miss MxG
missmxg.com
Miss MxG
Miss MxG
be brave

make it work. No one can bring this down. It's all about what I do. And it will have an immediate reaction to the outcome for my business.

If I have a plan B with another option, if Fempro Armor doesn't work out, then I'm not one hundred percent behind my product, and believe in what I do. So for me, I don't need a plan B.

You have had a fairly extraordinary life, tell a about coming to Australia.

So I told I was 19 when I told my mom on a Monday that I want to go to Australia and that I made an appointment with the Australian embassy in Bon. I'm originally from Germany. The following Friday back then the east west wall was still up. I asked my mom to come with me and we drove up to Bon. We sat in the embassy for about two hours and I walked out with my permanent visa, which was to a surprise.

I didn't think it would go that quick. However, being a good swimmer Australia at the time they wanted good swimmers. On the way home, we stopped at a travel agency, just to check out when flights go and there was one the following day. So I left on the Saturday and I arrived on the Monday with a one way ticket. I could not speak enough English to hold a conversation. I had three contacts that I needed to choose a trainer from at the time, because that was one of the conditions to get the permanent visa that I swam for Australia.

If you were to speak with other women and who were wanting to set up their own businesses, what would you recommend? How should they go about starting, do you have any words that you might like to suggest to them?

Oh, one big thing that has helped me is to surround yourself with people that are better than you. Ultimately you become what your five most people are as such. Yes. So if there are people that strive for better things it will rub off. Having a network and not being afraid of asking for help. I ask help each day, I did it today when I called someone in the US, because we want to launch into the US market. People in general want to help. So for me, if someone asks me, can I help someone? Of course I'm going do that because someone helped me. It's a great way to give back. And I find the majority of people are very helpful.

It's about overcoming your own ego, and let other people guide you. I listen to people's advice. If it feels right to me, I probably will do it. If it doesn't, I will thank them for their advice. And then I do what I want to do because ultimately it is still my business. But the biggest thing is to surround yourself with good people. And, when people have asked me, how do you find good people? You just ask, and you keep asking. I think, the success of Fempro Armour comes to that.

I'm not basing what I'm doing, on what I get out. I'm basing my work on how I can make someone else's life better. It's more about the people. We wanted to create something that saves people's life in motorcycling. It was about impacting their lives, which then comes back to us anyway.

So I think if someone creates a business and it's all about what can I get out of it? I wouldn't say their on the path of failure but they are missing an enrichment. For me I'm excited when someone buys a product, because I know their lives are going to be in a much safer situation, if they are getting into an impact. And that is it's not the sale. It's more about, I'm so glad this person is now safer.

This interview with Stephanie Bofinger can be heard on the Hepburn in Conversation podcast.

It's About Telling a Great Story

Hepburn in Conversation with - **Ruby Schmidt**

Earlier this year, we were delighted to speak with Film Producer Ruby Schmidt and founder of production company, Toy Shop Entertainment. Ruby shares a little about her life as an Australian film producer, her passion for telling great stories, and some of the film projects she has worked on.

I always try to be honest about this. I'm a second generation filmmaker, so my mum makes films. I've grew up around that. She's in documentaries. So, when I was looking at what I wanted to do, film making was always there in the back of my mind.

I went and studied law because that's what you do when you trying to separate yourself from your family apparently. But then I went straight out of law into advertising and then creative advertising for an agency called Carbon Creative. I started doing more long form media content, which led me to Production Manage and Line Produce my first long form series for National Indigenous Television (NITV). And that was ironically working under my mum at WildBear Entertainment. But that basically led me to do what I do today.

In terms of my work and what I do, I'm passionate about telling great stories and sharing big ideas, I think because I love documentary, I love this space, and truth is far more interesting than fiction. So, I like to bring that sentiment into everything I do!

To me success is work satisfaction. I think success is what you know, what you cultivate – I don't think it's necessarily some arbitrary benchmark to put yourself up against to give the feeling you're achieving something. A sense of satisfaction in your workflow, because life is one day at a time. Some days I feel really successful, other days I don't. But it's still part of an ongoing process to feel like I'm achieving something every day.

In 2020, while were still in year one of the pandemic, work felt very strange and I think this has something to do with where I was in my project workflow. I had just finished a documentary which premiered at Mardi Gras Film Festival and three or four weeks later we were in a global lockdown. It was very strange, very jarring. I felt my work momentum completely evaporate.

SYDNEY
FILM
FESTIVAL

s For Visiting
OORLIE - BOULDER

So that year I had one project finished and released, and one project in post-production. And then towards the end of 2020, we started to get back into this new normal. I was traveling, I went out filming in Kalgoorlie in December. And then 2021 it happened all over again and it was horrible. There was all these snap lockdowns, random border closures. Melbourne went into their long lockdown.

I was in Sydney about two weeks before that city went into their big lockdown. It basically killed the momentum again. You couldn't film anything normally, or barely shoot interviews. For one project some interviewees couldn't even get into the city because of things like the 'ring of steel' around Melbourne or simply because of the border restrictions and work moving them interstate.

In 2021 I was also working with a lot of remote crew. There was an editor who was working in two hours south of Sydney and a director in Canberra, and the rest of the production in Brisbane. So when all the borders shut, it was just a nightmare for creativity and workflow. The knock on effect, not being able to have the editor and director in the same room, access archives or even get archive delivered just caused so much disruption. I think one of the biggest issues for filmmakers in the pandemic has actually been how much it stifled creative flow.

The marketplaces that we usually go to as a filmmaker were virtual. Suddenly you didn't run into people anymore; you didn't talk to anyone in passing – it was all digital rooms. The sharing of ideas and the cultivation of great projects didn't happen during the pandemic. Thankfully, we are now back to face to face and there's honestly no replacement for it. You just don't have that natural creative flow when you can't be together in person.

I balance my film making between running my own business and contracting as a producer and production manager for hire. This is really common in the industry, it enables me to offset my low (or no) paying independent work. It's particularly important for me in my business, if I'm working on a project that's delayed, I can take on more contract work. Having that access to workflow has been really good. I had a few slow months at the start of this year!

In 2022 my work really picked up again. It's just gone crazy, which is good. I think it's promising that, given the pandemic, things have turned around. I think that is a general sentiment showing everywhere. But the aftereffects of the pandemic are still transpiring. Knowing it's going to get better keeps me positive and people around me are confident as well. The projects keep coming in!

I don't really work much in scripted film. For me, I have mostly worked on documentaries and archive driven projects. That was really fortunate during the lockdowns – it meant that my work was insulated in a way, but then other things were impacted. I'd usually go out and pull up some old microfilms, meet and collect paraphernalia from collectors and organise scans. Thankfully can now do all that again!

My philosophy on starting your own business, is I literally think it's a case of just jumping in. And you know all those slogans ring true, like 'just do it', or 'jump in, feet first'. You are going to make mistakes, but it's so worth it. It's really satisfying to go in and go, ' yeah, I'm doing this', and 'I'm going to do that' – it's all up to you! The downside to running your own business are the mundane things like your insurance payment is due, it's tax time again, all your accounts. But even with that, it is very satisfying when you pull something off because of everything you've done, and with film, it's satisfying to see your production company in the credits!

I've done two projects Under Toy Shop Entertainment. The first one was a documentary called 'Belonging', and that followed the parallel story of a young activist, Sam Watson, and activist called Rodney Croome, who has instrumental in gay rights activism in Australia and particularly in Tasmania. The story followed them as they looked at how Tasmania went from being the last state to decriminalize homosexuality, to becoming one of the most progressive states in the country, and probably also in the world, in terms of human rights. That was a really satisfying film to work on with Matt Scholten, the Director. Very beautiful story, really beautiful talent. We had that premiere at Mardi Gras Film festival and it went to Melbourne Queer Film Festival. It got a really great response. And then it went on to play on Channel Ten, which was really exciting.

The second film was with Director, Brodie Poole, who I'd worked with before on a pilot for a travel show. The film follows a gold prospector who runs for mayor of Kalgoorlie in 2019. It was just the most visceral thing I'd ever seen – a modern David and Goliath political battle set in regional Australia, with incredible subjects. We completed the film 'General Hercules' in late 2021. It premiered at Sydney Film Festival in June and went on to screen at Melbourne International Film Festival, CinfestOz and Brisbane International Film Festival. It was amazing. We were so curious about how audiences would respond to the film. With 'General Hercules' it is a very intense, very confronting film. It has a bit of humour in there, but it leaves viewers with a lot to think about. Thankfully the reception has been amazing – it's really kicked off a lot of interesting conversations.

The last project I did with WildBear Entertainment was nominated for an AACTA award for best documentary. That was 'Brock: Over the Top' – a feature documentary about the motor car motor racing legend, Peter Brock, who passed away in 2006. That was with Director Kriv Stenders and Editor Tania Nehme. It was a real privilege to work on that project.

I've learnt starting the production company is a marathon, it's not a sprint. There's no overnight success. The average development time for a full project is something like seven years in television and film production. It's a slow chip away, its lots of ideas, it's really cost prohibitive. Even though you can film something on your phone these days, it costs a lot to make broadcast quality productions.

The industry is a real test of resilience and a case of being prepared to be knocked back repeatedly. It is living on a minimum wage because you push all resources into a project, because once you get traction, then things will hopefully pay off. It's definitely not down to luck, it's all work, it's persistence, it's doing the work to generate the workflow. The creative industries are an absolute slog!

Reflecting on the impact of COVID, it probably did give me a better daily work structure. I exercise nearly every day now, I have an Apple watch that reminds me to periodically stand up, which is a good thing. Before I would spend a lot of time at my desk, sometimes working from 8:00am to 7:00pm before finally getting something to eat.

I definitely still get up and do spreadsheets after dinner and I might work on a project until late in the evening, but that works for me. I'm not a nine-to-fiver. I'm so much more functional in a stop start environment. Running your own business, you never forget about work either. I am constantly switched on in some capacity.

I now have a miniature schnauzer called Raf – he gets me up gets me up and away from the desk and my partner also has a better work life balance than me. That has also influenced how I manage my time – I am grateful for his good influence!

This interview with Ruby Schmidt can be heard on the Hepburn in Conversation podcast.

Meet the Featured Women

Jacqueline Hodges

Jacqueline Hodges is a Business Adviser, Chartered Accountant and Financial Planner. She holds a Bachelor of Commerce, a Diploma of Financial Planning, a Master of Entrepreneurship and Innovation, and a Master of Tax Law. She left the larger top end of town firms to begin a career as a business and tax law writer.

Missing the client contact she commenced running her own successful financial practice advising clients across Australia and together with a few international investors. She is the Editor in Chief of 10 Ellen Media overseeing digital magazines and other publications.

Early in 2020, the seeds of a publication to help promote her clients began to grow. This publication soon blossomed into a digital magazine aimed at women who were seeking business and career success.

The first issue of Hepburn magazine was launched November 2020, in the offices of 10 Ellen Media. Jacqueline has since then helped bring to print stories featuring many amazing women.

Twelve months after Hepburn's first issue, Jacqueline felt compelled to improve Women's Financial Outcomes and a new magazine WFO was launched in November 2021.

Jacqueline's love of people, business acumen combine with a creative drive to bring business and financial knowledge to women, through a network of contributors who aim to inspire and help women be their very best.

Sally McGrath

Sally McGrath, workplace wellbeing expert, author, and transformation coach is known for her innovative approach to individual & workplace wellbeing programs.

Sally works with some of Australia's most recognisable companies on employee wellbeing, retention, and engagement.

She has led teams and managed businesses working in high-pressure environments for 25 plus years from SMEs to large corporates.

Her programs have helped employees, teams and leaders enjoy better work / life synergy and productivity.

Sally's private coaching is to empower women to prevent burnout taking over their work and life, to stop being stressed out, burnt out and using "busy" as a badge of honour, by reframing their approach to the toxic overworking culture present in the workplace.

Sally's article first appeared in Hepburn magazine's 2022 issue 1, Radiant Edition.

*This article has been republished in the Hepburn 2022 annual. You can read Sally's inspiring **Plan Your Year Ahead** article on page 11.*

Caroline Bellenger

Caroline Bellenger is a passionate life coach, motivational speaker, and creator of 'Be The Impossible'. She is the recent winner of The Gold Coast Women of The Year Wellness Warrior & National Roar Award Best Advocate For Mental Health.

Caroline epitomises the philosophy of overcoming trauma through wellness and courage. From childhood sexual abuse to over twenty years of addiction and mental health issues, Caroline got sober in 2009. Since then, Caroline has achieved incredible success in life and business.

A few of her remarkable achievements include representing Australia in Triathlon at 50, climbing to Everest Base Camp, and going back to university in her 40s.

After a successful corporate career ended through workplace bullying at the age of 48, she took back her life by becoming a successful entrepreneur with several businesses.

Among Caroline's qualifcations are a Bachelor Social Science (Honours), NLP Master Practitioner, Domestic Violence Certificate, and Global Coaching & Speaking Authority - Speaker and Presenter Certification.

Caroline's article first appeared in Hepburn magazine's 2022 issue 11, Courageous Edition.

*This article has been republished in the Hepburn 2022 annual. You can read Caroline's **How to Find the Best Version of You** article on page 16.*

Emma Gierschick OAM

Emma Gierschick OAM is a survivor of both family violence and breast cancer and the fulltime carer for young daughter with Down syndrome.

Prior to being a carer, she was employed fulltime in various management roles.

She has received multiple awards or recognition for her work in each field, including being named as one of the Top 100 Women of Influence by AFR, named as Woman or the Year, and being recognised in the Queen's birthday honours list of 2021 with a Medal of the Order of Australia.

Emma has spent many years campaigning about family violence and the rights and vulnerabilities of children with a disability. She is lobbying for greater options for carers.

Emma's article first appeared in Hepburn magazine's 2022 issue 10, Duantless Edition.

*This article has been republished in the Hepburn 2022 annual. You can read Emma's **Life's Backpack Full of Mystery** article on page 20.*

Jean Adams

Jean is an Empowerment Coach and Business Mentor. She is obsessed with empowering women in their 50s, 60s, and 70s to joyfully and confidently step into their magnificence so that they can achieve their dreams and goals for their business and their lives, especially in times of change and transition.

She is an expert in adapting quickly to business and life transitions, having spent over 30 years working in numerous industries and careers, as well as having lived in many different towns and cities, throughout New Zealand and Australia.

This has given her a depth of experience that enables her to equip the women that she mentors, with the tools, habits, and strategies that empower them to move forward with courage, confidence, and clarity so they can transform their business, and their life, and achieve success on their terms.

Jean mentors women throughout Australia and New Zealand, online via Zoom.

Jean's article first appeared in Hepburn magazine's 2022 issue 8, Empowered Edition.

*This article has been republished in the Hepburn 2022 annual. You can read Jean's **The Joy of Reinventing Your Life** article on page 28.*

Lauren Sherson

Lauren Sherson is an entrepreneur educator, has a passion for psychology and research.

Most recently was a candidate in the Victorian State Elections standing for the seat of Albert Park. Lauren has previously run as a candidate in the Local elections standing for the seat of Melbourne.

Lauren holds a Master of Entrepreneurship and Innovation from Swinburne University where after she secured her first lecturing post.

Later she moved to RMIT to continue lecturing in Entrepreneurship. Over her career in Entrepreneurship Education she has met thousands of students, helping many bring their projects to fruition of their start up.

She has recently studied Psychology at the University of Melbourne.

Lauren is now growing her next venture, with her focus on local advocacy through events and media.

Lauren's article first appeared in Hepburn magazine's 2022 issue 10, Dauntless Edition.

This article has been republished in the Hepburn 2022 annual. You can read Lauren's ***It's All About Community*** *article on page 34.*

Dr Red Ruby Scarlet

Dr Red Ruby Scarlet is an activist, artist, early childhood teacher-researcher, consultant and academic. She has been working in the early childhood sector for more than 25 years and is dedicated to creating imaginative and inclusive practices that promote dignity and integrity in early childhood. Red has developed curriculum and learning frameworks nationally and internationally. Her published works highlight stories of the numerous research projects she has led and contributed to across the world.

Red is currently the Creative Director of Multi-Verse, an organisation that focuses on creating professional development and resourcing for early childhood—topics include arts, anti-bias approaches, inclusive pedagogies and curriculum.

Red also teaches part-time at Clovelly Children's Centre in Sydney, NSW. She plays a leadership role in the Social Justice in Early Childhood group and is the founder of the Social Justice in Early Childhood Foundation.

Tina's article first appeared in Hepburn magazine's 2022 issue 10, Dauntless Edition.

This article has been republished in the Hepburn 2022 annual. You can read our story ***Meet Dr Red Ruby Scarlett*** *on page 40.*

Julia Zielke

Julia is a Sales Coach who specialises in bringing ideas to life. She has spent 20years in sales, 4 years exploring coaching techniques and 2 years as a qualified Results Coach.

Julia is a highly experienced sales professional. She has spent more than 20 years working across the retail, media and medical industries. She has been trained, in sales, by some of the largest organisations in Australia, including News Limited, Johnson and Johnson and Ego-Pharmaceuticals.

Julia knows how to harness the power of humanconnection to build strong, long lasting relationships with clients. Julia's passion is bringing ideas to life. She uses a combination of selling strategies and neuroscience coaching techniques to help Business' generate consistent profit.

With a Science degree, a Business degree and a neuroscience based Coaching qualification, Julia is well placed to balance the strategic needs of a Business with human needs.

Julia's article first appeared in Hepburn magazine's 2022 issue 5, Tenacious Edition.

This article has been republished in the Hepburn 2022 annual. You can read Julia's ***Oxygen or Sales: the Business Dilemma*** *article* *on page 46.*

Alice Huang

As a consulting COO, my job is to learn the project as soon as possible. Once I know the project well enough, then I find out what is the ultimate goal for the project. It is my job to figure out where the gaps are so I can close those gaps from where we are to where we want to be.

Alice grew up in Vancouver, Canada and spent 2011 to 2016 living in Melbourne, Australia. She has extensive experience in real estate consultancy, operations, marketing and sales. She has been able to adapt easily to living in eight countries in her adult life due to her adventurous and open spirit. She now resides in Montreal, Canada.

Alice has worked for PropTech and HealthTech startups in the UK, Germany, Mexico. After Mexico City, Alice moved to Texas and co-founded a boutique real estate development company which currently has a team of 10 employees. She manages the company remotely from Canada.

She has now launched a crypto consulting business on helping launch blockchain projects.

Alice's article first appeared in Hepburn magazine's 2022 issue 2, Evolution Edition.

This article has been republished in the Hepburn 2022 annual. You can read Alice's ***How to Succeed in the Cryptocurrency Industry*** *article* *on page 50.*

Phoebe Dray

As a Certified Practicing Accountant and Business Finance Success Coach, Phoebe Dray is equipped to help you find clarity in your business numbers.

Phoebe comes from a place of experience. Prior to her current consultancy, she was a business owner, just like you. A partner of MGA Accountants, Phoebe was able to scale the business to double its size before successfully selling the firm in 2015. So when it comes to business, she knows the struggles, the need to hustle and what's required to succeed and achieve optimal outcomes.

Phoebe's mission is to help entrepreneurs and business owners navigate the road to business success with confidence and knowledge. Phoebe, with a clear focus on numbers and strategy; is on a mission to guide passionate entrepreneurs, just like you. To truly understand your numbers, eliminate business overwhelm and enable you to share your genius with the world, with a profitable, scalable business that allows you to live the life of your dreams.

Phoebe's article first appeared in Hepburn magazine's 2022 issue 12, Joyous Edition.

This article has been republished in the Hepburn 2022 annual. You can read Phoebe's ***Financial Literacy: The Missing Piece of The Puzzle in the Fight for Gender Equality*** *article on page 56.*

Rachel Lounds

Rachel Lounds is a Confidence coach and Imposter Syndrome Specialist helping women overcome self doubt and imposter syndrome to reach their career and personal goals.

She is a licenced associate of The Imposter Syndrome Institute, the worlds #1 source of imposter syndrome solutions, to deliver the Rethinking Impostor Syndrome™ program,

It is Rachel's mission to help professional women bridge the confidence gap to become to excel professionally and personally.

Rachel loves helping her clients power up their potential to ditch self doubt, find their purpose and maximize their careers and lives through 1:1 coaching, group coaching and interactive workshops

Rachel's article first appeared in Hepburn magazine's 2022 issue 6, Enriched Edition.

*This article has been republished in the Hepburn 2022 annual. You can read Rachel's **Imposter Syndrome: What it is and Why We Should Care** article on page 60.*

Georgina Pazzi

As an educator and thought leader for over three decades, Georgina Pazzi has continually found innovative ways to ensure all learners succeed. Her passion for making a difference has led her to discover many important fundamental principles in education that successfully shape the way for student learning and wellbeing growth.

Eventually creating 'edumazing' which originated as an idea in 2002. The name was founded through her desire to find and create amazing ways to support all students to love learning and life.

Many years ago, Georgina also coined the term 'Human Literacy' in education, as she realised it represented what is at the heart of how we can sustainably improve our learning, wellbeing and lives. This has shaped the work she does to lead transformational learning and teaching opportunities with schools, families, businesses, universities and organisations we work with.

Her years in digital leadership have also been a strength in developing future-proof learning communities. Students are empowered to be entrepreneurial, empathetic, and proactive citizens, creating a greater impact in their world as change-makers.

Georgina's article first appeared in Hepburn magazine's 2022 issue 12, Joyous Edition.

This article has been republished in the Hepburn 2022 annual. You can read Georgina's ***Mindset Intelligence*** *article on page 66.*

Spring Leahy

Spring Leahy, is the founder and Jewellery Designer of Magpiette (pronounced 'mag-pie-eht'). Magpiette is a fine jewellery company, based in Sydney, that is focused on mindfully creating and curating beautiful jewellery with meaning.

Spring has always been passionate about creating and working with her hands, and had tried many different creative hobbies before finding silversmithing just over 10 years ago.

Spring has a desire to create jewellery that holds special meaning for its wearer - whether that's a reminder of a person, place or milestone - rather than creating just another accessory

Our interview with Spring first appeared in Hepburn magazine's 2022 issue 12, Joyous Edition. Spring first wrote about jewellery trends for 2023 in Hepburn magazine 2022 issue 11.

*This interview has been republished in the Hepburn 2022 annual. You can read our **Meet Spring Leahy** article on page 75.*

Sarah Lloyd

Sarah Lloyd is a Sydney based fashion designer producing timeless designer pieces for the style conscious woman of today. Designed and made in Australia, the label's signature aesthetic embodies sophistication with a focus on quality and classic design.

Before focusing on design, Sarah worked with leading fashion designers, including the late Carla Zampatti and Leona Edmiston. She gained industry experience and an understanding of the lifestyle needs of the modern Australian woman.

Drawing on experience, she designs both ready to wear collections and bespoke pieces. She designs with the customer in mind, to create confidence through a refined selection of timeless foundation styles.

Sarah hosts intimate events from her studio inviting women to preview new pieces and find out more about the eponymous label. The studio doubles as a show- room for women to book private appointments, preview collections, and try on designs and discuss bespoke designs.

Our interview with Sarah Lloyd first appeared in Hepburn magazine's 2022 issue 4, Ambition Edition.

*The interview is republished in the Hepburn 2022 annual. You can read our **Meet Sarah Lloyd** article on page 80*

Chamani Weerasekara

Chamani Weerasekara, is the founder and designer behind the namesake, purpose-driven label CHAMANI.

Chamani designs for conscious luxury, and wearable activism.

Through her designs she fights for the freedom, equality and opportunity for marginalised women, girls and communities through timeless, thoughtful wearable art.

Her design is to create more than a brand or a label but to create a movement.

She partners with talented artisans to create beautiful custom hand-dyed and hand-woven fabrics using sacred and ancient techniques passed down through generations.

Our interview with Chamani first appeared in Hepburn magazine's 2022 issue 8, Empowered Edition. Chamani first wrote about her eponymous label and sustainable fashion in Hepburn magazine 2022 issue 7.

This interview has been republished in the Hepburn 2022 annual. You can read our ***Meet Chamani Weerasekara*** *article on page 86.*

Sallyanne Astill

Sallyanne Astill is a Brisbane based fashion designer. She started her label Astille in 2018 after finishing a (fourth) degree at Torrens University in Brisbane.

Sallyanne spent many years in the tech industry as a software engineer and feeling a little like a sore thumb as someone fashionable in a digital world where she was surrounded by corporate suits or tracksuits and hoodies.

She dreamt of following her passion for travel and culture through the lens of a fashion designer.

Astille was born and is now a ready to wear label inspired by the old Hollywood silhouettes reimagined in a modern world, made from beautiful fabrics and prints. Each collection she designs is created from a French inspired theme that is woven into every seam and in house designed print.

Our interview with Sallyanne first appeared in Hepburn magazine's 2022 issue 10, Dauntless Edition. Sallyanne first wrote about the Astill label and transeasonal trends in Hepburn magazine 2022 issue 9.

*This interview has been republished in the Hepburn 2022 annual. You can read our **Meet Sallyanne Astill** article on page 92.*

Cathryn Mora

Cathryn Mora is a Book Coach and Publisher based in Brisbane. She helps coaches, speakers and aspiring thought leaders write and publish beautiful self-help books, business books and memoirs.

A quality book will raise your profile, and attract new opportunities such as speaking, media, podcasts and new clients, because it ultimately positions you as a thought leader, and adds credibility and income to your business.

Through a genuine and practical approach to book writing and coaching, Cathryn encourages and empowers her authors to tell their own truth, grow their own business, and make an impact on the world.

Cathryn's portfolio of published collaborative anthologies written with your coaching students include, *Medicine Woman, The Path, Letter to My 10-year-old Self, I Fly,* and *From Passion to Leadership.*

Cathryn's article first appeared in Hepburn magazine's 2022 issue 6, Determined Edition.

This article has been republished in the Hepburn 2022 annual. You can read Cathryn's own story ***Publisher and Author*** *on page 102.*

Tasha Doucas

Tasha Doucas is a self-published author of her instructional book The Feminine Carer. She has a wealth of experience to share after caring for her parents, her husband and her son.

Tasha is currently caring for her husband through his cancer journey and their teenage boy diagnosed with ADHD. She now achieves everything she sets out to achieve with more.

Recognising the need to help and support other women, Natasha has created the Resilient Carer Program.

Tasha's article first appeared in Hepburn magazine's 2022 issue 12, Joyous Edition.

*This article has been republished in the Hepburn 2022 annual. You can read Tasha Doucas' **The Resilient Carer** article on page 108.*

Tina Haywood

Tina Haywood is a proud Yupungathi/Gangalida woman and a strong resilient woman. Tina shares her personal story in her book We Are Warriors, which she shows women to regain their power and not be afraid to make the decisions that truly matter.

Tina biography explores her life of living with domestic violence and suffering from sexual assault and child abuse trauma as a child at 7 years old, going into the Australian Defence force, through to becoming a mother, mentor, survivor and overcoming continuous adversities.

Recognising the need to support and empower others, Tina has created the BluebutterflySkye program to embue hope in those impacted by Suicide, and specifically the Indigenous/ ATSI community, Youth and DV victims.

Tina's article first appeared in Hepburn magazine's 2022 issue 10, Dauntless Edition.

This article has been republished in the Hepburn 2022 annual. You can read Tina's ***Turning the Table*** *article on page 111.*

Stephanie Bofinger

Stephanie Bofinger is the founder and inventor of FemPro Body Armour. for female motor cyclists.

Stephanie with her passion and drive has developed her seed of an idea into an international business. Today Fempro Body Armour protects active sportwomen not only throughout Australia but across the globe.

Stephanie a former Olympian swimmer immigrated to Australia at the age of 20 with very little English but with a strong determination to succeed.

She lives her life, has no Plan B and has enjoyed some truly interesting experiences, including riding on a sand bike across the Simpson Dessert in 2019 to raise money for Dolly's Dream in the charity event.

Stephanie doesn't believe in a Plan B, rather she believes you must give everything you have to focus on what you are doing now.

Stephanie's article first appeared in Hepburn magazine's 2022 issue 8, Audacious Edition.

*This article has been republished in the Hepburn 2022 annual. You can read Stephanie's article **It's All About Their Safety** on page 116.*

Ruby Schmidt

Ruby Schmidt is a screen practitioner and producer creating factual and scripted content. Ruby completed a Bachelor of Laws in 2013 before spending two years as a Development Executive at Carbon Creative, working across a diverse slate of projects including 'League Nation Live' (NITV), and 'Sesame Street Season 47' interstitials.

Ruby has worked as a Line Producer on the four-part NITV/FranceTV series 'Elements' (2018) for WildBear Entertainment and was the Production Manager on the MIFF/Netflix feature documentary 'Iron Fists and Kung-Fu Kicks' (2019). She was an Associate Producer on the AACTA nominated feature documentary 'Brock: Over the Top' for Universal and ABC.

Ruby is the founder and principal of Toy Shop Entertainment – a production company based in Brisbane. In early 2020 Toy Shop produced 'Belonging' a half hour LGBTQI documentary for Screen Australia and Ten Play which premiered at Mardi Gras in February. The film was awarded best Documentary short at Melbourne Queer Film Festival.

Ruby's film credits include General Hercules (2022), Belonging (2020), and the television mini-series Lindy Chamberlain: The True Story (2020).

Ruby's article first appeared in Hepburn magazine's 2022 issue 10, Courageous Edition.

*This article has been republished in the Hepburn 2022 annual. You can read Ruby's article **It's Telling a Great Story** on page 122.*

Subscribe to Hepburn

https://hepburnmag.co

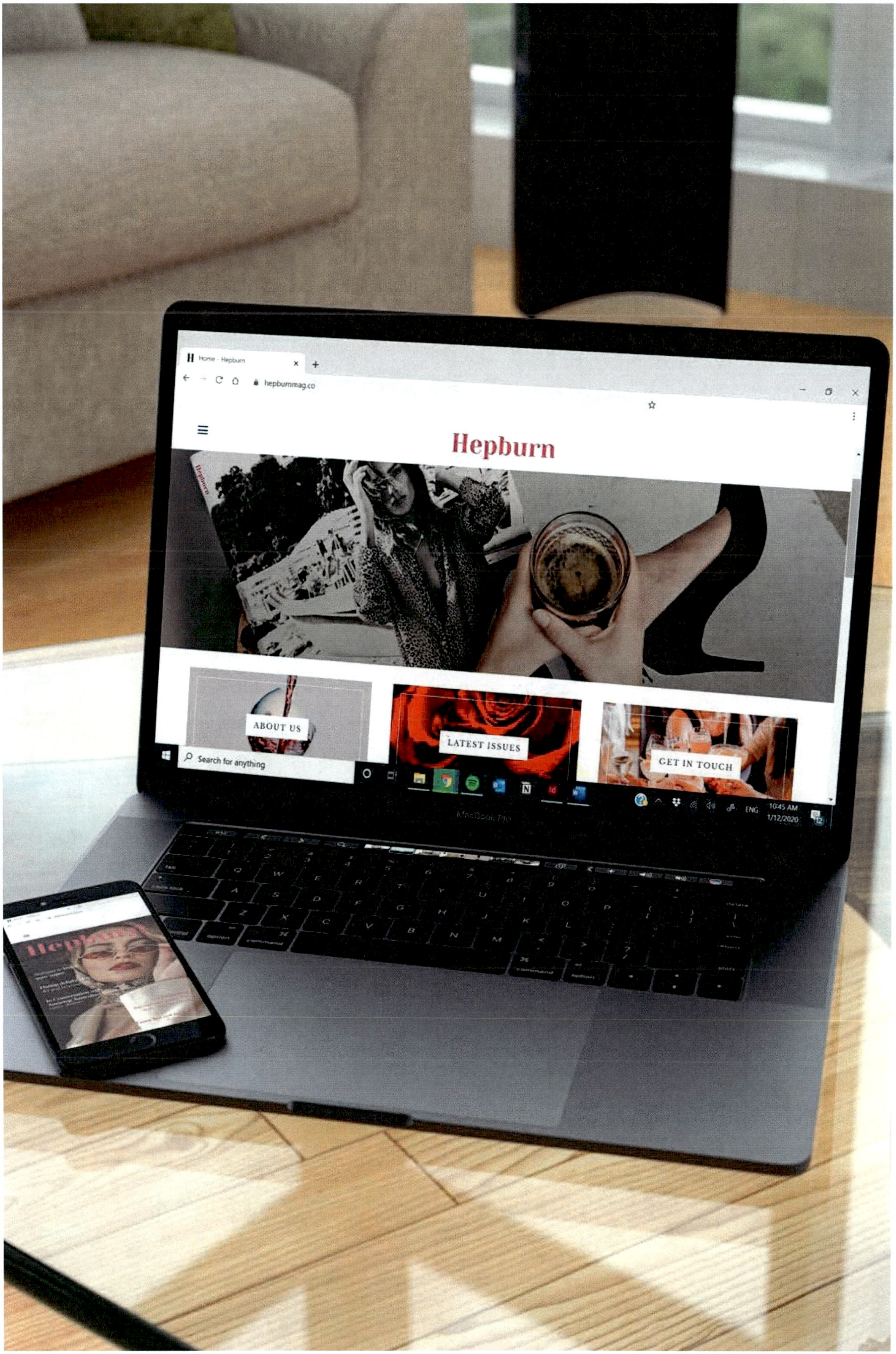
Home - Hepburn
hepburnmag.co
Hepburn
ABOUT US
LATEST ISSUES
GET IN TOUCH
Search for anything
ENG
10:45 AM
1/12/2020

About 10Ellen

10 Ellen Media is a privately owned, vibrant and youthful company that includes a portfolio of print and digital content. Based in Ipswich, Queensland, 10 Ellen Media reaches to national and international readers of all life stages.

Our work reflects our values of living in total harmony with ourselves and those around us while indulging in pleasures every now and then. We inspire our readers to seize the little moments of joy while working, cooking, traveling, creating, and just being.

Our creative teams collaborate with the readers and industry professionals to share their stories, creations, and beautiful ways of living and learning. The readers enjoy access to our work in their preferred channels that include print and digital articles, podcasts, social media groups, and video content. We welcome the experiences of our readers to create a community of like-minded people who share common interests and goals.

Our portfolio includes print and digital content inspired by the simple pleasures of life, wellbeing, travel, food, creativity, and community-building.

Our Portfolio

wfo

Hepburn

Embrace

TRAVEL YARNS

DILLYDALLY

Notes

Notes